Praise for *Gra*

In an unhealthy culture there is a desperate need for biblically centered healthy churches. My good friend John Jenkins has given us an informative practical tool in his book *Grace to Grow* to help churches and their leaders to build and sustain ministry that God can use to bring kingdom healing to a sick society.

> **—Dr. Tony Evans,** president of the Urban Alternative,
> senior pastor at Oak Cliff Bible Fellowship

Reading books on growing churches is a big part of my job. I love people who love to grow churches. Yet it's unusual to get a book like this—written by a pastor who has led a church to be one of the largest and most influential churches in the country. I'm grateful that pastor Jenkins distilled his wisdom into this book to help pastors and others navigate the many challenges and opportunities facing the church. This is not theory, but a lived, practical guide for the church today. Read it with your whole team!

> **—Ed Stetzer,** PhD, dean, Talbot School of Theology

This book carries the sacred weight and wisdom of a man who has modeled its message for four decades. The personal and public life of Pastor John K. Jenkins is steeped in a humility, grace, and integrity that reflects the depths of his relationship with Christ, his deep love for the church, and his desire to invest in its leaders. In these pages, you'll find insights that will sharpen your leadership, recalibrate your priorities, and reignite your passion for your calling. Pastor Jenkins's personal and ministerial reflections in each chapter are priceless, and they will serve as a guide to the reader for years to come. Gratefully, I have been a personal beneficiary of his generosity and counsel. And now, through this book, you can be too.

> **—Priscilla Shirer,** Bible teacher and author

If you want to know what it takes to grow a large *and* healthy church, this is the book for you. Pastor John Jenkins offers seasoned, practical, biblical, and values-driven advice that will help any church leader lead better. I encourage you to let him guide you and your team into a better understanding of the nuts and bolts of a real-life ministry. Doing so will impact both individual lives and communities for God's glory.

—**Dr. Larry Osborne**, author of *Lead Like a Shepherd*,
pastor of North Coast Church

When we see a magician perform amazing tricks, we always want to know how he did them. But magicians rarely reveal their secrets. When we see a church that has grown and grown for more than thirty years, we want to understand how that's possible—especially when many churches are struggling to stay afloat. *Grace to Grow* is a how-to manual for church growth written by Rev. John Jenkins, someone I have come to know as a "master pastor." This book lays out the solid ministry principles that ultimately lead to a growing and healthy church. Every church leader in America should read this book. It's that good.

—**Richard Stearns**, president emeritus of World Vision US, author
of *The Hole in Our Gospel* and *Lead Like It Matters to God*

Grace to Grow captures powerful, practical, biblically based lessons utilized by one of the nation's most successful pastors and churches for those seeking to grow impactful ministries. From his amazing pastoral leadership journey, Pastor John Jenkins provides a compelling must-read for pastors seeking to make church relevant in a culture and generation turned off to church but hungry for Christ's saving grace and love.

—**Dr. Barbara Williams-Skinner**, president of Skinner Leadership
Institute, co-convener of the National African American
Clergy Network, author of *Leadership Led by God*

Powerful, practical, and personal—listen and learn from the words of a highly effective church statesman. John Jenkins invites us to the gold standard of church excellence.

—**Leith Anderson**, author, president emeritus of the National Association of Evangelicals, founder's chair of World Vision International

Pain has purpose. My friend Pastor John Jenkins isn't wasting his experiences in the often painful crucible of ministry. In *Grace to Grow*, he shares the highs and lows with gripping candor and refreshing transparency. You will learn, grow, and share this pragmatic resource with all ministry leaders you know.

—**Sam Chand**, leadership strategist, author of *Leadership Pain*

Having worked with over 500 of the finest leaders of our generation, I can confidently say Pastor Jenkins is one of the wisest men I have ever met. In this book he generously shares some of his wisdom to help you grow into your full potential as a Christian leader! I have already ordered twelve copies to share his wisdom with my friends!

—**Bobb Biehl**, life coach, consultant, executive mentor

If anyone is interested in a healthy church, biblical tools on growing a church, and grace to grow, Pastor John K. Jenkins is a must-read. From learning humility, to the value of vision and mission statements, to establishing integrity, this book will equip, empower, and encourage every church planter, every senior or lead pastor, and anyone who is seeking a model on how to set up your church to grow gracefully.

—**Dr. Jasmin Sculark**, lead pastor, Victory Grace Center

John Jenkins is the real deal! Having grown up in church, having served in a small church, and then having grown a small church into one of the largest churches in the country, John Jenkins has earned the right to share with great authority how other pastors might grow their churches as well. Built on a foundation of grace and humility and loaded with personal stories of both success and failure, John directs us not only in how to grow a church but also in how to lead people to spiritual maturity. For any pastor who desires to move his church forward, *Grace to Grow* serves as a great blueprint to follow.

—**David N. Ashcraft**, president and CEO, Global Leadership Network

Grace to Grow

Grace
to Grow

*Creating a Healthy Church
in Unhealthy Times*

JOHN K. JENKINS SR.

FOREWORD BY T. D. JAKES
AFTERWORD BY WILLIAM D. WATLEY

ZONDERVAN REFLECTIVE

Grace to Grow
Copyright © 2023 by John K. Jenkins Sr.

Requests for information should be addressed to:
Zondervan, *3900 Sparks Dr. SE, Grand Rapids, Michigan 49546*

Zondervan titles may be purchased in bulk for educational, business, fundraising, or sales promotional use. For information, please email SpecialMarkets@Zondervan.com.

ISBN 978-0-310-15149-4 (audio)

Library of Congress Cataloging-in-Publication Data

Names: Jenkins, John K., author.
Title: Grace to grow : creating a healthy church in unhealthy times / John K. Jenkins, Sr.
Description: Grand Rapids : Zondervan, 2023.
Identifiers: LCCN 2023012999 (print) | LCCN 2023013000 (ebook) | ISBN 9780310151180 (paperback) | ISBN 9780310151203 (ebook)
Subjects: LCSH: Church growth. | Evangelistic work. | Church development, New. | BISAC: RELIGION / Christian Living / Leadership & Mentoring | RELIGION / Christian Ministry / General
Classification: LCC BV652.25 .J45 2023 (print) | LCC BV652.25 (ebook) | DDC 254/.5—dc23/eng/20230526
LC record available at https://lccn.loc.gov/2023012999
LC ebook record available at https://lccn.loc.gov/2023013000

The author is represented by Tom Dean, literary agent with A Drop of Ink LLC, www.adropofink.pub.

Cover design: LUCAS Art & Design
Cover photo: © Delphotos / Alamy Stock Photo
Interior design: Sara Colley

Printed in the United States of America

23 24 25 26 27 LBC 5 4 3 2 1

Contents

PART 3: BUILD UP GOD'S PEOPLE

PART 4: BUILD A CONNECTED COMMUNITY

Foreword

I know of no one like Pastor John K. Jenkins Sr. I've never seen such greatness clothed in such utter humility. I'm so proud to provide spiritual covering and support for him, which is itself further evidence of his humble persona. I mean seriously, how does one cover someone whose finesse is unrivaled, accomplishments unparalleled, and whose influence transcends race, politics, and denominationalism?

Pastor Jenkins does not say things he doesn't mean. He's a first-class individual. I have found him to be of impeccable integrity. Anyone can act in front of a crowd, but if he tells you something, you can stand firm in it. It's solid. It's real.

It's obvious why God blesses this man—because God can trust him. God can't trust some people, but Pastor Jenkins is an amazing person of integrity. His integrity is inescapable.

I've conducted huge conferences, and often, I did not even know he was there. Because he was in a back corner wearing blue jeans and busily taking notes. He never asks for a VIP seat. In most any crowd, he represents the largest church, but he has the smallest requests. He is good to everybody. He will help anybody.

Pastor Jenkins has always been willing to serve in silence and in secret. He pours out of himself to everybody, all the time. He never tries to be impressive. He never complains when his name isn't called out in public. In fact, in all the years I have known him, I have never heard Pastor Jenkins complain about *anything*. Ever. Not once. He demonstrates a level of integrity and humility that we have not seen in the kingdom in a long time.

Pastor Jenkins always shows up in simplicity and purpose and never makes a fuss. He makes being humble look good. While others are pushing to get to the front of the line, Pastor Jenkins sits in humility in the back of the room—head bowed, tears rolling down his face, thanking God for what he has done with two fish and five loaves of bread. For growing something small into a miracle.

Pastor Jenkins pours all of those admirable qualities into this book, and he shows how they can lead to a healthy and flourishing ministry, no matter its size. I know that many of you reading this book represent smaller churches and ministries. I believe this book will inspire you to keep shining brightly from your corner of the world. When we are small in our own eyes, God will bless us. When we are small enough to hold the door for someone, small enough to help and serve people in humility, he will bless us. I pray this book will inspire you to keep "doing small." Small is the new big, and it looks good on you.

I hope and pray that God will speak to you through this

book. That the words you read will shine a light on your life and minister to you in some divine way. That God will use this book to answer questions you have laid before you. To do something amazing with *your* two fish and five loaves.

BISHOP T. D. JAKES

Introduction

In 2017, First Baptist Church of Glenarden, Maryland, celebrated one hundred years in ministry. At the time, I marveled at our church's size and scope, given its humble beginnings. I still feel the same way today.

I first stepped through First Baptist's doors when I was nine or ten. My mom took me to church, and she never forgot my words as we drove into the parking lot: "We're not going into *that* raggedy building, are we?" I don't recall making that comment, but I trust my mother's account. She was a God-fearing woman, full of integrity.

While my words were less than gracious, they were honest. In those days, First Baptist was what some people would call a shack. A shack with a steeple and a bell. There were only a few windows, and the siding was dilapidated. The "restroom" was an outhouse.

It was not the most inviting building, but my mother, in her calming voice, reminded me, "We are not here for this building; we are here to worship God." And in that ragged building, we did worship. I joined First Baptist while still a child, and I grew up in that church. I have many fond memories of that time in my life.

I served as an usher and sang in the choir. I came to understand the importance of the church as a community. The people there became like family to me.

My favorite thing to do at First Baptist was to observe (and admire) Pastor John W. Johnson. When I was fourteen, I approached Pastor Johnson and revealed that I felt God calling me to preach the gospel. He told me I was a bit young for such a calling, but he encouraged me to keep praying about it. That's exactly what I did.

In 1972, our building was condemned and torn down. Under Pastor Johnson's leadership, we built another facility, and in 1973, we moved in. During that time of change, Pastor Johnson made a courageous decision. He licensed me, a fifteen-year-old boy, to preach. I delivered my first sermon in December of 1973. It lasted all of six minutes. Many of you reading this book might not know me well, but anyone in my current congregation will assure you that 1973 marked the last time I finished a sermon in six minutes!

In 1987, I was called to pastor Union Bethel Baptist Church in King George, Virginia, halfway between Washington, DC, and Richmond. This was a far cry from the church community I was used to.

At the time, First Baptist was a good-sized suburban church with hundreds of members. And it was just a short drive from my home. By contrast, Union Bethel was a rural church whose congregation measured in the tens rather than the hundreds. And it was fifty-five miles from home, more than an hour's drive each way. On a good Sunday, attendance might be as high as thirty-five people. On Easter, we could even reach fifty! It was discouraging; it was a tough season of ministry.

I made the drive to King George twice a week: Sundays for the worship service and Thursdays for all nine people who showed up for Bible study. On those Thursday drives, I would pass several of our member families, sitting on their porches and waving to me. It was clear that Bible study was not on their agenda for the evening. After studying the Bible with my nine attendees, I would drive home. Most of the families I had passed earlier were still outside enjoying the evening. They waved at me again.

Yes, Union Bethel Baptist Church was a tough place to do ministry, but it was a great training ground. One of the important lessons I learned there was how to deal with difficult people. Let's consider the case of "Sister Jones." If I told her, "Go right," her response would be, "No, I want to go left!" Everybody has a Sister Jones in their church, maybe even in their family. Sister Jones kept me on my knees, praying. I pleaded, "Lord, help me!"

Because I traveled to King George only twice a week, I spent hours on the phone with Sister Jones and others. And those were long-distance calls. I spent a lot of money trying to help Sister Jones and others understand what I was trying to accomplish. It was frustrating—and expensive.

Things came to a head when I decided to remove the artificial flowers that had adorned the pulpit area for many years. Those flowers were dirty and ragged, and they needed to go. As it turned out, those flowers had been placed by Sister Jones's grandmother decades previously. Their presence meant a lot to Sister Jones, and she had a conniption fit over their removal. As you might guess, she didn't come around the church after that. (When I eventually left this church, Sister Jones promptly announced that she would return to the congregation.)

Through my experiences with Sister Jones and others, God helped me understand that I was trying to use logic to convince people of *spiritual* matters. I was reminded of Jesus's words in John 3:3: "Unless one is born again, he cannot see the kingdom of God." So, I changed my strategy. I focused on teaching biblical principles instead of trying to debate people into following them. I served that church in King George for almost three years. Yes, it was frustrating, but my experience at Union Bethel Baptist helped make me the leader I am today.

I share these early experiences because I want you to know that I haven't always been the pastor at a megachurch. I started in a place very different from where I serve today. I understand the challenges and dynamics of a small church in a rural community.

In 1988, Pastor Johnson died of a heart attack. He had made it clear that he wanted his replacement to come from within the ranks of the church community. As a result, after interviews and a congregational vote, I was called to be the pastor of First Baptist Church of Glenarden in October of 1989. My official pastorate began the final Sunday of that December.

We started experiencing growth immediately. I must confess that the early growth spurt was due more to who I was than anything I did. I was a new, young pastor who also happened to be homegrown. I had grown up in this church, and a lot of the congregation knew me, so they welcomed me back. Another factor in the early growth was the curiosity that is sparked any time a well-established church welcomes a new pastor.

This growth forced me to think innovatively, for a variety of reasons. First, we quickly ran out of space. We could not squeeze another chair into the sanctuary, and it was not feasible to purchase the surrounding property. So in 1992, we purchased a home improvement store. A place where people had shopped for tools and resources for building homes and fixing broken things became a place where God provided tools and resources to souls that needed fixing. We "built out" that store (transforming a retail space into a church) with cash plus a mortgage, which we repaid in six years. We accomplished this feat by adhering to biblical principles on finance that I will share with you in chapter 7.

Shortly after settling into our new space, we outgrew that as well. (Do you see a pattern here?) On Sunday mornings, we needed overflow rooms—lots of them. At one point, we seated more people in the overflow rooms than in the main sanctuary.

Fast forward to 2007, when we built our Worship Center, where our services are held today. This $62 million facility includes 4,000 seats, 2,000 parking spaces, and forty-four classrooms. It sits on 160 acres. We paid half of the construction costs before we held our first service. Since moving into that facility, we have continued to grow.

Prior to COVID-19, our Sunday attendance averaged 11,000 over the four services we offer. On an average Sunday, one hundred people give their lives to Christ. Yes, every week we see at least one hundred people come to the altar to become believers in Jesus, rededicate their lives to him, or join our church.

I'm not sharing all of this to be boastful. I am painting a picture of our growth so you can believe that you too can experience healthy and meaningful growth—in your ministry, in your business, and even in your personal life.

In this book, I'm going to share the foundational principles of building an effective and vibrant ministry. It's important to note that when I talk about growth in this book, I mean much more than financial growth, increases in church attendance, or soaring popularity on social media. Are we as leaders growing *disciples*? Are we meeting needs in our communities? Are we growing in love for God and for one another?

Many of this book's principles apply to growing a church or ministry *and* to nearly every area of the Christian life. Whether you are a new church member, ministry leader, pastor, or business owner, you can apply these principles to build a life, ministry, business, or organization that honors God and positively affects people's lives.

What are the secrets of healthy, meaningful growth? That's a question I have been asked more times than I can count.

I am not special, and while I love my congregation at First Baptist Church of Glenarden, neither are they. What God has done for me and our church, he can do for you. I believe this with every fiber of my being. Most of what we have experienced is simply God's amazing grace. His goodwill. His pleasure. His favor.

However, we know that faith without works is dead. I would be remiss if I failed to share the practical lessons I have learned as God has given me and our church the grace to grow. As you will read, our church has faced challenges and setbacks. But we have strived to *persevere*, be faithful, and make the most of the grace God has demonstrated toward us. I highlighted the word persevere in the previous sentence because true and lasting success in ministry is not a quick fix. You can do things the right way and not realize success—or at least not immediate success. You can probably think of several churches who succeeded (at least numerically) without focusing on sound principles of Christian leadership.

And we all know churches that seem to be doing everything right but struggle to survive, let alone thrive. A church body is like a human body. You can eat right, exercise, and see a doctor regularly and still suffer from poor health. However, you will have zero chance of being truly healthy if you fail to follow the principles of good health and fitness. Principles do matter.

You may be surprised to learn that I am a private pilot. As such, I've learned the four dynamics of flight: lift, thrust, weight, and drag. I have found that if everything is in order— the lift is greater than the weight and the thrust is greater than the drag—the plane will get off the ground one hundred percent of the time. I started taking flying lessons in 2001, and I've *never* experienced a plane fail to take off. When I get to the right speed, I pull back on the yoke, and the plane takes off. Nothing else is required because everything else is in order. Church growth operates the same way. Of course, there are times when it's not advisable to fly, such as during strong crosswinds. There are "maximum allowable crosswind components" for various types of planes, runway conditions, and airport locations.

In other words, both pastors and pilots can face challenges beyond their control. However, I believe that if sound principles are in place, your church will tend to grow. Your business will grow. Your life and ministry will grow in ways that transcend mere numbers. Unfortunately, I've discovered that many churches lack the necessary principles that facilitate and allow for growth. That's a problem. When a ministry is not structured to handle growth, God will not allow it to grow in the ways that matter most. Further, without the right structure in place, a church can be overwhelmed by growth, especially numerical growth.

Over the years, I've learned to make changes that allow for growth. When I began pastoring, our church was not structured for growth; it was structured for tradition. It was structured to keep the current members happy. So I knew I would need to make changes. And once I started applying the concepts I'm going to share with you, the ministry changed for the better. Since then, it has advanced in more ways than I could have imagined.

Not only have I seen these concepts work in my ministry, but I have many spiritual sons and daughters to whom I teach the same things. As a result, these principles are helping their churches and ministries grow too.

So, that's my goal for this book: to tell you about building an impactful ministry and show you how you can apply these principles in every area of your life. In the following pages, I'll show you where God has taken our ministry and our church, and the lessons I've learned along the way. Thank you for joining me on this journey.

Part One

Build a Firm Foundation

Chapter One

Walk in Humility

Before you can fully understand and apply the principles I'm going to share, you must understand grace. No matter who you are or what your God-given assignment is, God gives you a measure of grace to handle and fulfill his purpose for your life. When I reflect on my life, I realize I cannot do anything through my own strength. I need God's supernatural ability to help me in everything I do.

Without God's grace, I wouldn't have built the courage and fortitude required to become a preacher at age fifteen. Without God's grace, I would not have accomplished or experienced all he has allowed me to achieve.

God's grace has put me in positions I am not qualified to hold. His grace has seated me at tables where I never would have been invited to sit otherwise. I've found myself in rooms with presidents, dignitaries, bankers, and executives—all by God's grace. I have seen many racial barriers broken. I have been in situations where I was the only Black person in the room, yet God gave me favor to be among people with whom I could connect and partner.

Not only did God give me the grace to handle every opportunity, but he also used those situations to allow me to form meaningful friendships that have blessed my life for many years. When our church began to outgrow what is now our Ministry Center, we were searching for property for our Worship Center. That is when I met Morty, a businessman who also happened to own the land we eventually acquired. When I discussed the purchase with Morty, I thought I could negotiate a lower price. But he stood firm. We bought the property at his asking price, but out of that transaction grew a wonderful friendship. Eventually, Morty invited me to serve on the board of his bank. So, a person who was never very good at math found himself sitting at the table with financial executives and experts! Go figure. Talk about God's sense of humor. By serving on that board, I was able to glean so much financial knowledge. Then I took what I learned and applied it to my life and ministry. My newfound knowledge wasn't the only benefit of this new relationship. God's goodwill toward us led Morty to create an endowment so children in our church who improved their grades could receive scholarship money for college.

This is just one of the countless examples of God showing

God's grace has put me in positions I am not qualified to hold. His grace has seated me at tables where I never would have been invited to sit otherwise.

me his favor and directing my steps. God wants to show you favor and direct your steps too, but it all begins with experiencing his grace. He wants to present you with opportunities and give you the grace to realize them.

Whatever God is calling you to do, he will give you grace to handle it. Most of us want to experience God's grace in our lives, but I've learned that too many of us expect grace for assignments we might want for selfish reasons—not the assignments God wants for us. One way to discern the true source of an assignment is to ask yourself this question: Who will this assignment benefit? Me and my career, or other people, especially other people who are in need?

For example, God does not give everybody the grace to pastor a 10,000-member church or even a 5,000-member church. If this were the case, who would lead the thousands of small- and medium-sized churches? God may be calling you to something different, so remain open to his will for your life and ministry. All of us should operate to the best of our abilities right now, with the grace God has given us. If you do this, God will empower you and present you with opportunities to be what you are supposed to be and do what you are supposed to do.

Now that you know the value of operating in God's grace, you are probably wondering how you can experience it for yourself. The key is humility. Humility is realizing that I can do nothing in my own strength. The Bible says, "God opposes the proud but gives grace to the humble" (James 4:6 NLT). When people tell me they want to walk in God's grace, I encourage them to walk in humility.

Philippians 2:8 reveals how Jesus humbled himself: He modeled humility by dying for us, and we should follow his model of self-sacrifice. We must be willing to give our all to fulfill our God-given assignment. So, if your ministry is about edifying or exalting yourself, that is not going to work. I do not know the specifics of what God has called you to do, but I can tell you without question that it requires dying to yourself. For example, I encourage pastors to take a look at their church website. Do the photos and videos feature the pastor and other members of leadership, or do they feature people from the church membership (especially volunteers, who are often underappreciated) and the community at large? This is one way to determine what a church's priorities are and the message it communicates to its community. On a similar note, listen to your sermons from time to time. How much do you talk about yourself, especially in glowing terms, versus the time you invest honoring others, telling their stories, and giving the ultimate credit to God?

James 4:10 promises us, "Humble yourselves in the sight of the Lord, and He will lift you up." Similar verses abound in Scripture. God is crystal clear, and he doesn't mind repeating himself on this topic.

Humility is the doorway to receiving God's grace. That's why it's the key to being effective in all facets of your ministry. For example, in a later chapter, I will address humility's importance in conflict resolution.

If we humble ourselves, we avoid getting to a point where God has to humble us. That experience can be painful, and its consequences can linger for a lifetime. In the pages ahead, you will read about some of my own struggles in this area. None of us are perfectly humble all the time. The good news is that when we are *intentional* about having a spirit of humility, God will show us favor.

Humility is important in its own right, but it also builds other character traits, like patience. First Peter 5:6 encourages us, "Humble yourselves under the mighty hand of God, that He may exalt you in due time." I love that verse because it highlights the importance of having patience as you walk in humility. You might not get all of the results you want right away, so strive to develop patience while God shapes you.

When you consider the qualities of great leaders, you will find that humility is a common character trait. Moses, for example, was considered one of the greatest leaders, and the Bible exalts his humility. Numbers 12:3 says, "Moses was very humble, more than all men who were on the face of the earth." You might recall that when God selected Moses to lead his people out of bondage, Moses replied, "O my Lord, I am not eloquent, neither before nor since You have spoken to Your servant; but I am slow of speech and slow of tongue" (Ex. 4:10). He asked God to choose someone else.

Because I have tried very hard to follow the example of Moses and other humble leaders in the Bible, I am very grateful that when people speak of me, more often than complimenting my speaking ability or leadership skills, they cite the character trait of humility. That's humbling indeed!

Many people have asked me how to stay humble. When they look around, they see so many people living wild, lavish lifestyles that appear devoid of humility. That's a road they want to avoid. Here's what I tell them: "I recognize that at any moment I could be homeless." Possessions and positions can be here one second and gone the next. So I do not focus on those things. I don't go into a room full of people and seek to be at the top of the list or have my name called out. I acknowledge when I am wrong. Sometimes, I accept the blame for something even if I am not at fault. I realize this might sound counterintuitive, but leaders must ask themselves, *Do I want to be "right," or do I want this ministry to be effective?* A leader bears ultimate accountability, so it's not disingenuous to say, "I could have handled that better" or "I should have done more."

Let's look for opportunities to serve, not to be served. Let's focus on solving problems, not assigning blame. In essence, it's all about servanthood—having a heart to serve people. Walking in humility is a lifestyle that every servant leader should embrace.

Humble leaders understand that growth and success are about so much more than numbers. Large does not equal effective. Please keep humility front and center as you read the rest of this book. I will share important growth principles with you, but my goal is not to teach you how to grow your own megachurch or raise your business to Fortune 500 status. Applying the concepts in this book does not mean that your church will suddenly explode to 10,000 members.

Rather, my goal is to share practices that will help you function wisely and efficiently, no matter the size of your organization. I want you to do humbly what you are called to do *well*. Anytime you do that, the by-product is growth, the kind of growth that is measured by much more than your balance sheet, social media presence, or attendance spreadsheets.

Chapter Two

Know Your Vision
and Mission

Before you can build an effective ministry, you must lay a firm foundation. The first step in laying that foundation is developing a clear vision and mission statement. Every person, family, and church should have a vision and a mission. Your *vision* should describe who you want to be and what you hope to accomplish. Your *mission* should describe how you will fulfill your vision.

A vision statement is vital because it guides and motivates. It helps define who we are and what we hope to accomplish. In a church, a vision statement leads and inspires current members and staff, and it helps prospective members (and prospective leaders) understand what that church is all about.

Imagine going to a concert where some of the orchestra is playing jazz, other musicians are playing classical, and a few others are doing opera. And no one seems to be playing the same song. I'm sure you can picture the confusion and frustration for the orchestra, the conductor, and the audience.

Proverbs 29:18 puts it this way, "When there's no vision, the people get out of control" (CEB). The King James Version uses even more stark terms: "Where there is no vision, the people perish."

When it comes to vision statements, I recommend starting on a personal level. Have you crafted an *individual* vision statement, describing what you see yourself doing down the road? And what is your personal mission?

Your personal vision, as well as your mission for your life, should spring from burden and passion. Some people view a burden as a negative, but when God places a burden on our hearts, it's an impassioned call to action. We see a need or an injustice, and we feel called to do something about it. We see a need for change, and we want to be God's agents for that change. Do you feel a sense of passion about something? That could be the burden God wants you to work on.

Your *vision* should describe who you want to be and what you hope to accomplish. Your *mission* should describe how you will fulfill your vision.

It's common to assume that all churches have a vision and a mission—some sense of who they are, where they are going, and how they are going to get there. We can read the mottoes on their websites or signage. However, as I have worked with churches over the years, I have found that many leaders don't truly understand what their church is all about or what their purpose should be. And if a church's vision and mission are not clearly articulated, it is foolish to expect growth.

Imagine this: Someone approaches you and asks you to make a sizable donation to their foundation or ministry. You ask important questions:

"Why does your organization exist?"
"What are your goals, and how will you
    accomplish them?"
"How, *specifically*, will a donation from my church help
    you fulfill your mission?"

If you receive no clear answers to your questions, will you support this organization? Probably not.

Recently, I was training a group of leaders from a church. I asked the group if anyone could tell me about the church's vision and mission. There were seventy people in the room. Only three responded to my question. And I received three different answers. That's a big problem.

Think about your church. If I asked the same question of your leadership team, are you confident that the responses would be accurate and consistent? If a church's leaders are not clear on what their organization is all about, how can they mobilize others to be a part of what they are trying to accomplish?

At First Baptist, anyone involved in our ministry will tell you that we are about discipleship. Ask one of our leaders, one of our members, or the church custodian, and you will get the same answer. They will tell you we are about making dynamic disciples.

This goal is evident in our vision and mission statement: "Developing Dynamic Disciples through Discipleship, Discipline, and Duplication." The first part of the statement represents our vision: *developing dynamic disciples.* Our vision is rooted in Jesus's command in Matthew 28:19–20: "Go therefore and make disciples of all the nations, baptizing them in the name of the Father and of the Son and of the Holy Spirit, teaching them to observe all things that I have commanded you." In a sense, Jesus has provided a vision statement that any church can follow. After all, "all nations" includes your local community.

The second half of the FBC statement (the mission) articulates *how* we fulfill our vision: *through discipleship, discipline, and duplication.*

Your mission and vision statements should work hand in hand. I know of a company that had a strong vision. It was about enriching lives and building relationships. However, the company's mission statement was all about increasing top-line revenue. This company struggled for years because its mission statement was weak on two fronts. First, employees were not motivated by a mission that centered on gross revenues. More important, the mission did not support the vision.

At FBC, our vision and mission statements are intrinsically connected. We strive to accomplish our goals by exposing people to God's Word and ensuring that we are accountable to each other as we apply the Word to our lives. That's where the mission statement's words *discipleship* and *discipline* factor in.

Our people will also tell you that we raise others up to take what they have learned in our ministry and pour it into others, again and again. That's what we mean by *duplication.*

DEVELOPING YOUR VISION STATEMENT

As I mentioned at the beginning of this chapter, I encourage you to avoid the temptation to build before a proper foundation is established. That foundation building includes considering these key questions as you create or refine your church's vision:

- What is our ministry's purpose?
- Who do we hope to be?
- What do we hope to achieve?

Your vision statement does not need to be complicated. At First Baptist, we were able to capture our vision in just three words. And here is an early version of Microsoft's simple vision statement: "A computer on every desk and in every home." Note how the Microsoft statement is short and simple and easy to memorize, but still manages to highlight the company's purpose and big-picture goals.

By contrast, here is a former vision statement from Hershey, the chocolate company: "Undisputed marketplace leadership." Points for brevity, but would you be inspired by this vision? What's more, this statement is frustratingly vague. Which marketplace are we talking about? What is meant by leadership? And how do you know if you are the "undisputed" leader of chocolate, or of anything for that matter?

Here's another way to tell if your vision statement (or mission statement) is lacking: If it could apply to virtually any business or organization, something is missing. If you removed your church's name from your vision or mission statement, would people still have a sense of what you are about? If your statement could just as easily apply to the local pet shop or bakery, something is wrong.

FROM VISION TO MISSION

Once you have discerned your church's vision, the mission comes next. Ask yourselves, "How is our church going to achieve our vision?"

The eight-word vision/mission statement of First Baptist Church of Glenarden was birthed out of my burden and passion to see people grow spiritually and become mature Christians. Developing dynamic disciples—that is what we want to see. How, specifically, are we going to do it? Through discipleship (helping people learn biblical truths), discipline (working those truths into their lives), and duplication (taking what they have learned and pouring it into others). These specifics are important, because people can agree on a vision but disagree about how to achieve that vision.

We'll explore discipleship in more detail later on, but for now it's enough to know that we have made discipleship the cornerstone of our church's vision and mission.

SHARING YOUR VISION AND MISSION

Once you've crafted a clear vision and mission statement, are you confident your leaders and the congregation share your understanding?

I share our statement because I want to encourage all churches to create a simple phrase or two that clearly communicates what you are all about. It should be easy to remember and share with others. I have yet to see a successful church where only a fraction of the people can articulate its reason for existence. Everyone in your church should be able to recite the vision and mission statement.

Teach your members to know and understand the vision and mission. Repetition is a great learning tool. Make sure people keep seeing your statement, keep hearing it, and keep repeating it. Over and over again. This is how they will learn it and put it into practice.

Everyone in your church should be able to recite the vision and mission statement.

At our church, people encounter our statement multiple times every week. They hear it during sermons and classes. It's part of our video announcements. We say it when we welcome guests. It's printed and displayed throughout the building. It's on our website and social media. I want that vision and mission drilled into the hearts of the people so they can understand discipleship and carry it out.

THE BLESSINGS OF STRONG VISION AND MISSION

If your church doesn't have a vision or mission statement, I hope this chapter will inspire you to create one. If you already have a statement, is it clear? Is it biblical? Are there specific Scriptures that support it? Is it accurate? Have you communicated it well?

Is it guiding what you are doing now, as well as your plans for the future?

Crafting a vision and mission statement helps a church assess its priorities. It helps leaders determine which ministry activities and other endeavors best achieve the church's goals.

At our church, we combined our vision and mission into one statement. However, there is nothing wrong with two separate statements, as long as they relate well to one another and are easy to remember. Here is the vision statement for Dr. Tony Evans's church, Oak Cliff Bible Fellowship in Dallas, Texas: "To have transformed lives that transfer the values of the Kingdom of God." Their mission statement is "Discipling the Church to Impact the World."

Here is another good example from New Beginnings Church in Matthews, North Carolina, whose vision statement is "Our vision is to praise, proclaim, promote, and protect by providing Godly principles." Mission statement: "Our mission is to reach people through God's love, God's Word, and God's hand."

Here's a key tip on this topic: Make sure your ministry priorities are aligned with your current fiscal and personnel resources. You might have to postpone or eliminate certain endeavors if you simply don't have the resources to do them effectively.

On a similar note, review your vision and mission statements regularly. Your goals might expand as your resources grow. And there might be other reasons to realign your priorities or identify new ones. Your community might grow exponentially. It might experience dramatic demographic changes.

It's more likely that your vision statement (assuming it's a good one) will endure, while the mission statement might need to be adjusted, but both should be evaluated regularly.

Please don't underestimate the power of a strong vision and mission statement. Clearly defining what your church is all about brings everyone together, working toward common goals.

Chapter Three

Establish Integrity

When you think of someone with great integrity, who comes to mind? Take a few moments to consider this question.

Did it take a while to come up with an answer, or did several people immediately pop up in your mind's eye? I picture my late father-in-law, James Donald Prather. He has been gone for a while now, but the soundness of his moral character still inspires me. He was truly a man of his word; his yea was yea, and his nay was nay. When he committed to doing something, he always followed through. He was a man you could depend on. His actions were based on his principles, which were, at their core, biblical principles. He believed in fairness, moral and ethical behavior, and personal responsibility. If you asked him why he was going out of his way to fulfill a commitment, he would say, "Just for GP." GP was his shorthand for "general principle." He established moral and ethical standards for his behavior, and he followed those standards, regardless of circumstances or consequences.

Because of these principles, he gave clear and honest answers, even if he knew those answers might be unpopular. He didn't beat around the bush. He governed his life by moral principles rooted in Christ. These principles never wavered, no matter how he felt or what he was enduring in life. His integrity was inspiring, and his candor was refreshing. I still miss him every day.

The integrity my father-in-law demonstrated is scarce in today's society, and that includes the ministry. This is most unfortunate, because integrity is vital to the development and success of any ministry or organization. Here is just one example of how integrity has eroded. For decades the Gallup organization has tracked how Americans rate the honesty and ethical standards of various professions. In 1985, 67 percent rated the honesty and ethical standards of the clergy as high or very high. By 2010, that number had slipped to 53 percent. In 2021, the percentage had dropped to only 34 percent.[1] As you will see later in this book, the lack of integrity among pastors and other ministry leaders is a major reason many people, especially younger people, are leaving the church.

Clearly, we need more integrity in our personal and professional lives. I believe the standards for Christian leaders have been lowered in recent years. As the Gallup research above indicates, people are aware the standards are slipping. However, too many parishioners tolerate bad behavior by their leaders. I have seen fatigue set in when a leader behaves poorly, lies about that behavior, and then, when those lies are exposed, concocts new lies to "explain" the previous ones.

Only when we make integrity a priority, pattern, and practice in our daily lives will we grow as people. When we live with integrity, others know they can trust us and have confidence in us. They will follow our leadership because we have shown them that we can be entrusted with responsibility.

Integrity is a simple concept, and everyone knows it's important. However, many leaders, including religious leaders, struggle to live and lead with integrity. As I write this chapter, high-profile pastors and ministry leaders are in the news for lapses in integrity. I fear the same thing will be happening as you *read* this chapter, many months from now. Are there more scandals today than there were twenty years ago, or are they just more visible because of social media and the wide variety of other sources for information? This question is up for debate, but I believe the internet age has created a host of new temptations that are available with a few clicks of a button or keyboard.

Consider how easy it is for a pastor (or anyone) to access pornography via a smartphone or laptop. Consider the number of affairs that have been carried out in the virtual world, where it's much easier to keep them concealed.

Some pastors take comfort in the fact that they have avoided major moral failures, but integrity is more than avoiding catastrophic public mistakes. How many of us have committed to doing something we lacked the time or energy to accomplish? How many times have we said we would attend someone's sporting event, concert, or birthday party, but failed to show up? And how many times, to secure a speaking gig, new job, or media interview, have we portrayed ourselves as someone we are not? Maybe fudged a resume or embellished our bio? These are all integrity deficiencies. Integrity is a character trait that shows up in the large things, the small things, and everything in between.

Integrity is more than avoiding catastrophic public mistakes.

Here's another integrity-related scenario I have seen several times: A church launches a building campaign and begins to raise money for a new or expanded worship center. But months pass and nothing happens. People wonder where their money went. It certainly didn't go toward new construction. And if there is no explanation from the leadership, people might assume their money ended up in the pastor's bank account (especially if he's suddenly driving a new car), or that it went toward some other project without their knowledge or consent.

True, there are no perfect people, but integrity in all things is still a worthy goal. And even if we believe integrity is one of our strong suits, we can all improve in this area. We should strive to do so.

Many of the problems we see in today's world spring from a lack of integrity in leadership. The daily decisions politicians, church leaders, and business executives make have far-reaching effects that they fail to consider in the heat of a moment. Whenever I see a leader crash and burn as a result of financial dishonesty or immoral behavior, I marvel at how different things could have been if more leaders had James Donald Prather's honesty and unwavering moral standards.

INTEGRITY IN THE CHURCH

This brings us back to the important topic of integrity in the church. Many people are leaving the church or becoming less involved. Here is the unfortunate reality: People do not want to be involved in church for a variety of reasons, but the lack of integrity among pastors and other religious leaders is always at or near the top of the list. Many people have heard countless examples of people with no moral ethics. Others have seen integrity failures firsthand.

We will explore the exodus of millennials and Gen Zers from the church later in the book, but it's worth noting here that, according to research by Lifeway, 66 percent of Americans ages twenty-three to thirty said they stopped regularly attending church for at least a year after high school. Seventy-three percent of this group cited pastor- or church-related reasons for leaving, and nearly one-third of this group specifically noted the church's hypocrisy and judgmentalism.[2]

Today's younger generations would rather avoid church than risk being under the leadership of a church that is not properly growing and developing because of dishonesty, corruption, or dishonor. I won't give specific examples, but I am sure you can think of more people than you can count on both hands who fall into this category.

Perhaps, as you read through this chapter, you will realize that your own integrity barometer is lower than you want it to be. I have good news for you! God can give you the grace to grow in this area of your life.

So, how do we develop integrity? First, we need to establish core values such as honesty. Let's commit to being honest and making sure the members of our team know they will be held to that standard as well. They should understand that we will not turn a blind eye to dishonesty.

Here's an example from my ministry: I once had an employee who was stealing from the church. We had evidence of what was going on, and I confronted this person about the situation. He lied right to my face.

It's important to note that when I learn that anyone on my staff has an integrity issue, I give him or her an opportunity to correct that behavior. In this case, I allowed the person to pay back what he had stolen. I also referred him to someone so he could get professional help. Unfortunately, a few years later, theft happened again, and I had to let the person go. This was a hard decision for me, but it was necessary.

Some integrity issues, like the one above, are overt. It is clear what has been done and who did it. But other challenges are not as clear-cut.

For example, evangelism is a core value of our church. Because of this, our leaders must be certified altar counselors. They are trained to lead people into a vibrant relationship with God by walking them through Scripture.

Each year, all of our leaders attend a retreat, and, during one of these events, I learned that several of my leaders were not certified altar counselors. This was another integrity issue, because each of these uncertified counselors had signed an agreement committing to meet *all* of the qualifications of a leader. On the surface, this might seem like a small matter. Perhaps some of them forgot to get certified; it merely slipped their minds. That is still an integrity lapse, even if it was not overt. When you sign an agreement, you need to follow up and ensure you are keeping your word. A promise is not something you can forget.

My first step in dealing with this problem was to hold certain department heads accountable, because it is their responsibility to review and approve all prospective leaders. Next, I required the uncertified leaders to make immediate arrangements to get certified. We set clear deadlines for accomplishing this task. And, praise God, they all came through!

INTEGRITY: PROACTIVE AND RESPONSIVE

The situation above illustrates that it's vital to address integrity issues immediately. If I discover that one of our leaders is demonstrating a lack of integrity, they either correct it or they're out of here! They're gone. We don't rush to judgment, and we act carefully and prayerfully. We have an employee handbook that everyone is expected to follow. And we have a code of conduct that all employees sign. It lists twenty-five specific actions for which someone may be dismissed immediately. (If you want to create your own code of conduct but aren't sure where to start, you can find First Baptist Church of Glenarden's Code of Conduct in the appendix at the end of this book.) And we have a leadership questionnaire form that every prospective leader must complete.

This might seem like a lot of paperwork, but I'm not going to let anyone damage our church's reputation and ministry. I'll say it again: A lack of integrity drives people away from a church. And for those who do stick around, it can keep them from forming deep connections with their church or fully trusting its leaders.

Leadership Questionnaire Form

Every leader must be a member in good standing:
Regularly attends worship and prayer services
Faithfully attends monthly Communion services
Committed to and *involved* in at least one ministry of the church
Active in a teaching ministry
Financially supporting the church through tithes and offerings

"Leadership only functions on the basis of trust" – John Maxwell

Ministry Name: _____

Ministry Position: _____

Nominee's Name: _____

Address: _____

City: _____ **State:** _____ **Zip Code:** _____

Phone Numbers: Home _____ Work _____ Cell _____

Email address: _____ **DOB:** _____

How long have you been a member of FBCG? _____ **Your tithing/offering #** _____

Are you employed? ☐Yes ☐No   **Are you tithing?** ☐Yes ☐No

Are you certified as an FBCG Altar Counselor? ☐Yes ☐No

List the ministries you are actively involved in: _____

_____   _____

_____   _____

What teaching ministries are you involved in on a regular basis?

☐ The Institute   ☐ Tuesday Bible Study   ☐ Wednesday Bible Study

☐ Sunday School   ☐ Discipleship Ministry (identify which ministry)_____

☐ Other _____

Leadership Training:
☐ Foundational Leadership Class
☐ Other: (any leadership training you have taken in or outside of First Baptist Church of Glenarden.)

_____   _____

_____   _____

☐ I certify that I am a member in good standings according to the above requirements and am eligible to be considered for a leadership position.

_____   _____
Date   Signature

That's why I encourage you to have systems in place that allow you to recruit people who *already* possess integrity. We must be diligent about vetting potential leaders. As many of us have learned firsthand, that is no easy task. But if there are questions about a candidate's integrity, that's not the time to take a chance and hope for the best. This is one reason our employees must sign and follow a code of conduct. We also do a background check and fingerprint any volunteers who want to work with our children and youth.

I realize that some small ministries might not have the resources for this level of safeguards. If that is the case for you, I encourage you to reach out to a large church or ministry in your community. Chances are, they will have such systems in place, and they should be willing to assist you. Our church does this all the time.

As a leader of a ministry, business, or any organization, you have a responsibility to address integrity issues not only within yourself but also with the people you supervise. Be as proactive as you can, but be willing to *react* wisely, swiftly, and definitively when you need to.

With your current leaders, examine them closely and guide them wisely. Our church's leaders are evaluated annually according to their job performance *and* their character. Those being considered for leadership are required to complete a series of training sessions focusing on those same two criteria. We do not put people in leadership until they demonstrate that they are living out the necessary qualifications.

For reference, here are some character-based requirements for leaders at our church:

1. They must regularly attend our worship and prayer services.
2. They must faithfully attend our monthly Communion services.
3. They must be involved in and committed to at least one of our church's ministries.
4. They must be active in a teaching ministry.
5. They must financially support the church through tithes and offerings.

I have seen churches make the mistake of overlooking integrity issues and putting people in leadership before they are ready. Perhaps it's because someone is a talented teacher or because a pastor fears that person might leave the church if he or she can't be a leader. I encourage you to avoid these temptations. You can't appoint someone to be a deacon and then hope he will, over time, develop the integrity to fulfill the necessary responsibilities. That's why we carefully examine the backgrounds and ministry history of all potential leaders. We talk with those who have worked with them. We look for patterns, both positive and negative. And we continue to monitor patterns of behavior *after* someone is hired.

At our church, we are committed to identifying people who are *already* walking in the attributes of a deacon—doing the things a deacon is supposed to do. That way, when we announce a new deacon, people do not hesitate to say "Amen!" They affirm our decision because they have watched that person live a life that shines with integrity.

With all of my heart, I encourage you to value integrity and apply it in all areas of your ministry. A lack of integrity can disrupt—and even destroy—what you have set out to accomplish. On the other hand, when you commit to living your life and fulfilling your ministry assignment with integrity, you give God the opportunity to grow and develop your church *supernaturally*. That's what he wants to do, but it can't happen without integrity. Yes, some churches might grow numerically, at least for a season, despite a lack of integrity, but do you think God will truly and deeply bless a church that continually defies the defining principles of his character?

Chapter Four

Create a Spirit
of Excellence

Picture this: You visit "Church A" for the first time. When you drive through the parking lot, you dodge potholes to avoid ruining your car's suspension—or spilling your coffee. The asphalt is overgrown with weeds, and it's unclear where you are supposed to park. The spaces were marked at one point, but the paint has faded to near invisibility.

You park your car and walk to the building, dodging those potholes on foot this time. You sigh with relief when you reach the sidewalk, but then you trip on a crack in the concrete and nearly face-plant.

You step inside the church, but there's no one to greet you or direct you where to go. You decide to use the restroom before the worship service, so you wander aimlessly until you find it, hidden in a dark corner.

You enter, only to find that none of the open stalls have toilet paper. You hope that the one occupied stall has supplies, and you wait awkwardly for it to become available. You fear the worship service might start without you.

Then, after you've finally done your business, you prepare to wash your hands. All of the soap dispensers are empty except one on the far end, which seems to have a drop or two left. Better than nothing, but not *much* better. You can barely work up a lather.

At this point, I probably don't even need to say much about the paper-towel dispensers.

After drying your hands on your pants, you make your way to the sanctuary. As you walk into the dimly lit room (some of the light bulbs have burned out), the ushers do not make eye contact, smile, or greet you. Someone merely hurries you to a seat. That seat is lumpy and torn. It leans to one side, rocking every time you shift your weight. You fear it's only a matter of time before it tips over or collapses.

When the service gets underway, you strain to hear the choir and the pastor over the outdated sound system.

Now imagine this scene: You visit "Church B." When you enter the parking lot, smiling attendants in bright, reflective safety vests direct you to a clearly marked space. You park and walk to the building, enjoying lush, manicured landscaping and smooth sidewalks along the way. As soon as you walk in the door, a greeter warmly welcomes you, and when you ask where the restroom is located, he provides clear directions, even offering to personally escort you.

You quickly and easily find the restroom, which is clean, bright, fresh-smelling, and fully stocked with everything you need, including multiple soap dispensers (filled with high-quality hand soap) and an abundance of paper towels. You notice comfort items like facial tissues and conveniences like hand sanitizer and baby-changing tables.

You make your way to the sanctuary, and a friendly usher greets you with a smile and helps you find a seat. Your seat is clean, comfortable, and *stable*. You can easily read your Bible and the bulletin and take notes under the warm, bright lighting. And even though you are seated near the back, you can enjoy the full, melodious sound of the choir and the powerful preaching via the state-of-the-art sound system.

Which church has earned your return visit? Yes, at Church B, you experienced *excellence*.

But let's dig a little deeper here. What if Church A is a place of anointing, vision, and mission? Isn't that important—more important than what some might call aesthetics? Here is the problem: People will miss what you, your church, or your organization are all about if certain things are done poorly, especially if those things are highly visible and form first impressions.

People get turned off when they are uncomfortable, ignored, or inconvenienced, or they witness a basic lack of care in the way a church presents itself. Some great churches struggle to grow because they don't strive for excellence in everything, including the so-called little things.

So what does it mean to strive for excellence? First, it does not mean that everything has to be *perfect*. Churches of all sizes have to prioritize resources, and ministry and service to others should precede aesthetics when push comes to shove.

Excellence means you pay attention to detail and are

constantly in pursuit of high quality. We always give our best, and our best might not look the same as the church across town. If you look up "excellence" in various dictionaries, you will find it related to other terms like "superior" and "first-class." That should be our standard. There is a big difference between giving our best and settling for our worst and hoping no one will notice. That attitude has given the church a black eye. When a church tolerates mediocrity, it is authorizing mediocrity to take up residence and make itself comfortable.

Let's "visit" Church B one more time. The leaders, staff, and volunteers there went above and beyond to make sure attendees enjoyed a great experience, from their arrival all the way through the worship service.

Everything was intentional, right down to the vests sported by the parking lot crew. Anyone entering the parking lot knew whom to ask if there was a question, such as, "Where are your handicap spaces?"

When you focus on excellence, people appreciate it because focusing on excellence means you are focusing on *them*. Visitors are likely to return, and they will tell their friends and family about the wonderful experience they enjoyed. That's one reason we strive for excellence in all aspects of our ministry. At FBC, we intentionally cultivate excellence in the way we serve within the church, within our community, and beyond. It's in our culture, in our DNA. Our mentality is, "If we can't do it with excellence, we won't do it at all."

I have visited churches all over the world, but I have seen only a handful that do everything with excellence. Most churches, regardless of their size or budget, can improve in at least a few areas.

So how do we put the spirit of excellence into practice? First, evaluate everything—from the parking lot to the pulpit. I am talking about every facility and every activity. Don't forget your website, advertising, and social media presence.

Second, for every item on your list, ask, "Do we excel in this area? If not, how can we make that happen?" As you review your list, you might find items you simply need to let go of—assuming they are not vital to your church's ministry.

Finally, think about examples of excellence you have seen, and don't limit yourself to other churches or ministries. When was the last time you were blown away by a business that did something incredibly well? How can you replicate that excellence within your organization?

When you do this inventory, you may realize that there are some things that must change, even if you can't resolve them immediately.

At First Baptist, we have more than a hundred ministries, many of which have been running for a long time. Occasionally, a ministry's leader steps down, and no one feels called to fill the void. I could ask someone to assume that role. (And most people will do what the senior pastor asks them to do, even if they don't really want to.) But I avoid this temptation. I don't want someone to lead because they feel pressured by me. A ministry works only if its leaders feel called to lead and possess the passion to do the job.

In cases where no one steps up, and I can't identify anyone with the passion and sense of calling, I decide to shut down the ministry until we find the right fit. This is hard to do, but it goes back to our commitment: "If we can't do it with excellence, we won't do it at all."

We will do a deep dive into leadership in part 4 of this book, but I want to note that having the wrong person at the helm of a ministry undermines excellence. It forces an organization to lower its standards.

Insisting on excellence in all things causes momentary discomfort and even disruptions in the services you want to provide. But it's worth it in the long run. Applying the excellence standard to every area of our organization has been vital to our growth and effectiveness. You can grow and succeed too!

If we can't do it with excellence, we won't do it at all.

I encourage you to review that inventory I mentioned earlier. Study each item on your list and imagine what your ministry could look like if you strived for excellence in every detail. Then, take the time to pray about what you need to do and the resources you need to find. For example, perhaps you have a new Sunday school teacher who is still finding his voice. He's giving his best but still has room to grow. What can you do to foster that growth? How can you train and encourage that teacher on his journey toward ministry excellence?

If the people or resources you need to accomplish a specific goal are not in place, the time to pursue that goal has not yet come. If God has given you the vision to accomplish something, he will provide what you need, but in his timing. And the result will be excellent.

Chapter Five

Make Your Motives Pure

Y ou know, Pastor, I really see our church growing to
three thousand members."

I laughed when I heard Deacon Lemuel Cousins utter those
words several years ago. He was a brilliant man (a biologist
by trade), but I was certain he was wrong. I chuckled and said
to myself, "How in the world could our five-hundred-member
church grow to three thousand?" And 12,000 members (our
current total) was so far-fetched it would have been embar-
rassing to even consider.

I never dreamed of pastoring a megachurch. My dream
was to impact people's lives so they would become passionate
followers of Jesus. This brings us to a vital principle for growing any organization: *Your motive must be to better the lives of the
people you serve rather than to serve yourself.*

For me, serving others meant directing people in their spiritual transformation. For someone else, service might mean developing a product or service that meets a specific need. Whatever the case, your emphasis should always be on others. Whatever you are doing in your church, ministry, or other organization, don't do it for selfish reasons.

If you launched a church to make a name for yourself and accumulate wealth, you are missing a very important principle. Philippians 2:3–4 reminds us, "Do nothing out of selfish ambition or vain conceit. Rather, in humility value others above yourselves, not looking to your own interests but each of you to the interests of the others" (NIV). The God we serve considers our outward behavior, of course, but also the condition of our hearts, as the Scripture above emphasizes.

HOUSTON, WE HAVE A HEART PROBLEM

How do we know we are truly focused on others? By examining our hearts. Take a moment to think about your inner self. What are your inclinations and intentions? What is your disposition? What are your ambitions, your short- and long-term goals?

As you answered the questions above, how many times did the words *I, me,* and *my* come up? If you, not others, were the focus of each answer, that might indicate a heart problem. And if that's the case, I understand. I have battled heart problems of my own. There was a season in my life when I chased status and the acceptance of others. I sought achievement so eagerly that I didn't realize how I was affecting my family (and all of my loved ones), as well as my health. I took on far too many preaching and speaking opportunities. It gave me the esteem and prestige I craved, but I eventually ran myself ragged.

More important, I neglected my family. My wife and my kids felt neglected, as if I didn't value them enough to spend time with them and minister to them the way I was trying to minister to the masses.

It's important to note that God was not the one directing me to assume all of those responsibilities and speaking engagements. I did it because I was chasing my own ambitions, and it got me in trouble. All of the activity took my focus away from God and my God-given assignment to develop people.

Through Scripture and through the way God interacts with us, he makes it clear that he wants our hearts to be pure and kingdom-focused. He doesn't want us to be consumed by our own selfish motives. Philippians 2:3 instructs us, "Let nothing be done through selfish ambition or conceit, but in lowliness of mind let each esteem others better than himself."

Here is my challenge to every pastor and ministry leader reading these words: Make sure your heart is in the right place. Make sure you are operating with pure, God-centered motives.

In today's churches, many people have impure motives. For them, it is not about the glory of God; it is all about "me." If we want God to use us for his glory, our hearts must be authentic. Those of us who are senior pastors must operate from pure motives and inspire other leaders (as well as laypeople) to do the same.

Here are a few hallmarks of people who demonstrate pure motives:

1. They are willing to do the hardest work.
2. They are willing to do the work that often goes unseen.
3. They seek no praise or acclaim for what they do.
4. When they are complimented, they give the glory to God and to others.
5. They ask, "What can I do to help others?" rather than, "What's in it for me?"

The successful ministries I know have created a culture where the focus is on developing others. For example, one of our church's leaders started with a ministry of five people and built it to more than 200. This woman had admirable personal initiative, but more important, her motives were pure, and she did it all for the glory of God. She showed up for people in their time of need. She celebrated their accomplishments, she prioritized developing their character, and she did so much more. She poured herself into people's lives.

She started the ministry as a layperson, and today she heads one of our church's largest departments, one that is focused on helping and serving our members and the community at large.

Every layperson in your church should have this kind of opportunity. If their motives are pure, they should be able to contribute to a successful ministry that makes your whole organization more effective.

As leaders, let's remember that we are not just building an organization; we are building *people*. We are striving to help people *be better*. We can impact the kingdom by ministering to them and helping them minister to others. God does not limit his glory to pastors and other leaders; he wants to use *everyone* to advance his kingdom.

So, how do we cultivate and maintain pure motives? Here is what I have learned during my many years in ministry: First, pure motives require *daily* discipline and self-examination. That starts by exercising restraint in my life so I can stay focused on serving God by ministering to people who are hurting.

Just because you can buy something doesn't mean you *should.* I have seen a materialistic lifestyle distort the motives of many ministry leaders. Wealth and its trappings can distract us from what God is calling us to do.

I encourage you to keep a close watch on your motives. Each of us must establish our own boundaries and stay aware of the specific temptations that pull us off course. When we lose our way, we need to make corrections and regain or sharpen our focus.

> **We are not just building an organization; we are building *people*.**

Here's something that has helped me. I strive to take nothing for granted. I remind myself every day that everything can be taken away in a heartbeat. I encourage you to acknowledge this reality too. It's a great way to be aware of what is truly motivating you. If you find yourself caught up in building a kingdom that is all about you, please remember that it can be torn down in a day, even in an hour. But the love and wisdom and compassion we pour into others can last a lifetime and beyond.

Second, remember that accountability and humility produce

pure motives. I've seen this over and over in my life. Everybody needs accountability.

Simply put, if you are not accountable to anyone, you are out of control. If you are a pastor without a pastor, you are headed for trouble. If you are a layperson without a pastor, you lack spiritual covering over your life.

As for humility? As I shared earlier, humility makes me realize that everything can be gone tomorrow, so I must do the right things—the things that honor God—*today.*

Without accountability and humility—without the daily washing of our hearts and minds with the Word—we cannot keep our hearts and our motives pure. I encourage every pastor and leader to have a prayer partner who holds you accountable for that daily washing. Having a prayer partner has been life-changing for me. I have been blessed by people in my life who ask me the tough questions and encourage me to examine my heart. I want you to experience that blessing. If you don't have a partner like this, please find one.

Our world needs more leaders with pure motives. We need people who will stand up and say, "It's not about me and my gain; it's about you and your needs."

Chapter Six

Cultivate Meaningful Relationships

God accomplishes his work on earth through people, and that's why it's so important to make meaningful connections with others. I like to say that relationships are the currency God uses to get his work done.

Take a moment to consider the richest, most supernatural blessings in your life. If you are like most people, another person (or group of people) helped to make each blessing possible.

Has a manager or coworker shown you special favor on the job?

Have you ever received an unexpected financial blessing from your church or fellowship group?

Has someone provided an exciting opportunity for your child—through sports, education, the arts, volunteer work, or something else?

Whatever the case, if someone has blessed your life, God moved a heart to make that happen. This is why I encourage you to avoid operating your ministry (or your life in general) as a Lone Ranger. You will struggle to grow and thrive.

However, when you cultivate relationships with the people God brings into your life, he will use those relationships to open doors and create opportunities to take your ministry to new heights.

When we take the time to get to know other people and share with them, we broaden our horizons. Relationships grow exponentially. If we build bonds with a few people, God will use those relationships to connect us with even more of his family— people we might not have met otherwise. I am confident God will use your relationships with others to help you fulfill his assignment for your life as long as you cultivate the relationships with pure motives.

Relationships are the currency God uses to get his work done.

Over the course of my life, I have been blessed with many incredible opportunities. I have traveled the world. I have preached to governors. I have preached to presidents. I have served as chaplain of an NBA basketball team. All of these opportunities sprang from the meaningful relationships I have developed over the years. It's worth repeating what I said earlier: Relationships are the currency God uses to get his work done.

I am living proof of this truth. Every significant ministry opportunity I have enjoyed has sprung from a relationship God has provided. Relationships have enabled my ministry to grow. Relationships have led me to be a part of my local business community, and they have allowed me to serve on the boards of various organizations, from banks to hospitals to global-impact organizations to church-planting coalitions to colleges and universities and so much more. Relationships are the root of it all.

On a personal level, many of my dearest friendships have happened the same way: One person introduces me to a good friend of his, and soon we are all close friends. I believe that everything (the personal and the professional) hinges on relationships. That's why we need to connect with people and cultivate friendships.

MY MINISTRY CONNECTIONS

Pastors Bert and Charné Pretorius lead an incredible, impactful ministry in South Africa. They founded 3C Church in Tshwane, South Africa, which now serves more than 30,000 members and has expanded to other cities in South Africa and beyond. They have become great friends to my wife and me. I met Bert when I traveled to South Africa to support my covering pastor, Bishop T. D. Jakes.

During that visit, my friend Israel Houghton introduced me to Bert. "I want you to meet my friend Bert Pretorius," he said. From that introduction, Pastor Bert and I developed a friendship. Over the past ten years or so, I have been able to preach and teach in South Africa almost every year.

Pastor Bert has introduced me to other South African church leaders, and I have been able to minister to their congregations as well. For example, Pastor Bert introduced me to Ray McCauley, senior pastor of Rhema Bible Church in Johannesburg. Pastor McCauley was influential in ending apartheid by taking a stand for righteousness. He defied apartheid laws and opposed injustice. His church was one of the first in South Africa to provide interracial church services. He invited Nelson Mandela to preach at his church while Mandela was still considered a controversial figure. Pastor McCauley played a significant role in working with the South African government to transition the country out of apartheid.

His legacy is truly remarkable. To this day, thousands of people attend Rhema every week. It's one of the world's most influential churches. Because Pastor Bert introduced me to Pastor McCauley, another friendship and ministry partnership has grown. I had the honor of ministering at Rhema during a celebration of Pastor McCauley's seventieth birthday and the church's fortieth anniversary. It was an amazing celebration, and I was honored to be one of the keynote speakers.

Relationships like these have changed my life. I've learned things that have opened my eyes to how the church can be more impactful. For example, Bert and Charné's ministry has a great discipleship program, and I've implemented their ideas and initiatives to help our church reach people and bring them to Jesus. The Life Groups at our church are modeled on the cell groups Pastors Bert and Charné created.

Here's how it happened: When you lead a large church like mine, you need to find a way to create smaller groups if you want to connect with people in a meaningful way and cultivate interpersonal relationships. After all, these close relationships teach us how to forgive, how to pray, and how to take care of one another. This is why I wanted to create cell groups within our church, but I was unsure of the best way to do it. When I saw Bert and Charné's model in action, it expanded my vision of what a cell group could be, and it gave me confidence that a similar model could work for the church I pastor.

After implementing Life Groups at our church, we immediately started seeing people getting more connected to one another, and these connections have been instrumental to our growth and effectiveness. I owe it all to God's leading me to a relationship with Bert and Charné and allowing me to see their ministry firsthand.

I should add that this couple ministers at my church almost every year, and they have planted several churches here in the United States. Our church supports these new ministries any way we can. It's another demonstration of how relationships lead to exponential and mutual growth.

I hope these examples from my life and ministry illustrate the importance of cultivating meaningful relationships. I give Pastor Bert so much credit, because he made the effort to contact me after Israel introduced us. He pursued a friendship with me, and our strong bond endures to this day.

I encourage you to do the same. Pursue relationships with people. Take the time to know them. Build a friendship; be relational. Once you have established a relationship, work to maintain it. Stay in touch. Stay connected. God will use these relationships to expand your horizons and help you grow, in all senses of the word. Your ideas and strategies will grow. Your ministry's reach will grow. Your impact will grow. And all of this growth will help you carry out your God-given assignment.

The first church I pastored (in King George, Virginia) came about because of my relationship with Pastor T. L. Rogers. In 1987, Pastor Rogers invited me to speak at this church, and those services must have gone well, because I was invited back. After that, the church asked me to be their interim pastor.

I declined this offer because I didn't want to give up the evangelistic ministry I was doing at the time. Then they asked me to become their permanent pastor. This time, I accepted. Again, all of it was birthed out of relationships and friendships.

Here's another example: In 1997, a local pastor friend named Bob Mathieu invited me to host a gathering for ministry leaders, informing them of an evangelistic event coming to the Washington, DC, area. I was somewhat reluctant to get involved, but I agreed to host the gathering. There, I met evangelist Steve Jamison, the co-founder and leader of "Jammin' against the Darkness," an outreach featuring NBA stars and Grammy-winning musicians. The event is now called Jamfest, and it features a three-on-three basketball tournament, a slam-dunk contest, and more. Steve and I have now been friends and partners in ministry for twenty-five years. Our families have bonded. I have preached at his church many times, and he has returned the favor. (Today, Steve is lead pastor of Eastridge Church in Issaquah, Washington, a multi-site church with two campuses in the Seattle area and one in Addis Ababa, Ethiopia.)

More important, my friendship with Steve is one of the most significant in my life. He is one of my dearest friends, and I have learned much from him. And I have been able to share my principals of ministry with him, something I know he appreciates. Our friendship continues to be meaningful and powerful for both of us.

KEYS FOR CULTIVATING FRIENDSHIPS

As you pursue and cultivate your own meaningful relationships, please be aware of your motives. I can tell when someone is pursuing me for an opportunity, not a real relationship. If you are approaching someone because you are seeking an opportunity, then you are merely an opportunist, not a friend. (I have met a *lot* of opportunists in my years of ministry.)

So, make sure your friendships are based on genuine care and love. Yes, meaningful relationships can lead to incredible ministry opportunities, but they should be valued and appreciated in their own right.

As you cultivate relationships, I encourage you to focus on those that align with your values. I encourage you to monitor relationships regularly, asking, "Who is influencing whom in this relationship? Am I risking my integrity in any way?"

In my many years of ministry, I have had to end only one friendship. But it had to be done. This person's values varied significantly from mine. For example, he was an opportunist (of the type I mentioned earlier). Everything was about creating opportunities for him, not others. He seemed to hold no regard for my best interests or those of his other friends. The things he said and did served his agenda. Have you been in a meeting in which someone's every idea, suggestion, or piece of advice is self-serving? Then you understand what I am talking about.

On the other hand, you know you are cultivating a real and meaningful relationship when a friend focuses on helping you and enabling you to serve others.

I must end with a warning, which I have alluded to a

few times in this chapter: Use discernment as you cultivate relationships. Keep asking yourself that "Who's influencing whom?" question.

Further, if someone shows you they cannot be trusted, consider whether they are the kind of person with whom you should develop a relationship. Healthy relationships help ministries and individuals grow, but unhealthy ones have the opposite effect.

Part Two

Build a Strong Infrastructure

Chapter Seven

Budget for Success

I realize that budgeting is not as exciting as some of the topics covered in this book. But it's vital to cover these functions, because they represent a huge challenge for churches of all sizes. In this chapter, we'll explore the importance of managing human and financial resources and provide a model that fosters growth and stability. I'll address these functions from the perspective of the church, but the principles I share will apply to any business or personal-finance scenario.

BUDGETING

Contrary to what some churches believe, budgeting is not something to hide from church members. They need to see what's happening with the finances. They need to see that their tithes and offerings are being used wisely.

If a church collects tithes and offerings but doesn't disclose how that money is being spent, it creates suspicion and distrust. For example, as I mentioned earlier, churches that have been amassing a building fund for years, even decades, but there's no new building. No improvements to the old building either. The ragged carpet hasn't been replaced in years, but the pastor is driving around in a new car. That's a problem—a budgeting problem and an integrity problem.

At our church, we have committed to sharing how we are putting tithes and offerings to good use. We seek every opportunity to show our members that their giving is making a difference. For example, we note that we give 10 percent of our income to various ministries and organizations because this is important to our church community.

> **Budgeting is not something to hide from church members. They need to see what's happening with the finances.**

We have "adopted" twelve schools, which we support financially. We also support our local chapter of the Boys & Girls Clubs of America. When disaster strikes, we partner with other churches and organizations to support relief efforts. We demonstrate to our members how our income is used to impact our community and the world at large. This inspires confidence in us. Our members know we use their contributions wisely and effectively.

Do you know what people are saying about today's churches? They are saying we don't benefit our local communities. They say we spend money on ourselves, not others.

Sadly, for many churches, they are right. It's time to change these perceptions. Here are a few ways to make it happen:

First, if a church expects its members to tithe, the church needs to tithe too. As you have just read, that's what we do at First Baptist. We provide funds that benefit our community, and that inspire our members to do the same. As I write this chapter, I'm giving thanks for being the pastor of First Baptist Church of Glenarden for more than thirty years. When I became the pastor, I started exploring opportunities to impact the community through giving. We have emphasized supporting our community financially, and we are not ashamed of it. We promote it. Over the years, God has blessed us so we can bless others—not only locally, but also nationally and internationally.

Second, we must understand the principle of the harvest. Many churches today expect to reap where they have not sown. Unfortunately, the principle of reaping a harvest does not work that way. If you expect to reap something, sow something. If your church embraces an opportunity to bless others, your church will be blessed as well.

I should note that our church did not always function this way. When I became pastor, our church had thirty-two "clubs," such as the Willing Workers Club, the Good Samaritan Club, the South Carolina Club, and so on. A major function of these clubs was an anniversary celebration. Funds were spent so a club could celebrate *itself.* Picture thirty-two afternoon anniversary parties every year, with around thirty-two people attending each party. This went on for years. Every club had its own budget and kept its own money. One club kept its money in a shoebox under "Ms. Bessie's" bed.

After I became pastor, the first thing I did was require all the various clubs and ministries to bring their funds to the church treasury. After all, this was the church's money, so it needed to be turned in to the church. It did not belong in anyone's personal bank account (or shoebox).

After all the funds were secured in-house, I required every ministry or club to develop a budget. I explained that we were a tithes-and-offerings church, so each ministry's budget would come from tithes and offerings.

This might seem like a no-brainer to some of you, but operating this way was a novel concept for our church back in the day. We had clubs raising money by selling Katydids candies or holding barbecues.

Other fundraising efforts included hosting trips to Atlantic City, the resort town famed for its casinos. Yes, our church used to sponsor trips to Atlantic City. People parked their cars on the church lot on Saturday morning and retrieved them on Sunday night after returning from the beaches, boardwalks, and casinos.

I quickly put a stop to that. We were not going to continue taking our church to Atlantic City. Shutting down this type of fundraising created drama, but it was necessary. I needed to move the church toward developing a centralized budget. We couldn't have a bunch of auxiliary ministries all doing their own thing.

Today, every ministry in our church must submit a budget request, detailing how they will spend their funds. All money is disbursed from a central budget, which helps ensure accountability and transparency. In our church, we have key checks and balances in place, but the senior pastor ultimately controls the budget. The budgeting committee makes sure our spending is in line with our budget. They carefully track our spending. The auditing committee makes sure everything is in order and provides an additional layer of accountability. The finance committee writes the checks, pays the bills, and manages deposits.

This system works well for us. We have lots of eyes on how money is spent and invested, but I, as the senior pastor, bear ultimate accountability. The buck, both literally and figuratively, stops with me. I believe this approach facilitates accountability and transparency.

If our church has to cut a program or eliminate a staff position, that final decision lands on my shoulders. I work with the committees noted above, and I seek input from everyone I can, but I am accountable. This way, there is no finger-pointing or blaming a committee or a few members of a committee.

This brings us to a third (and very important) principle: Even with a central budget in place, we still review all spending and strive to find ways to save money. For example, you can almost always find a way to cut fat from a budget. If one of our ministries requests an annual budget of two thousand dollars but spends only half of that, we don't give them two thousand dollars the next time around. They didn't demonstrate that they truly needed that much.

Here's another little secret I've learned about trimming your budget: Find discounts. I encourage you to look at every line item in your budget and seek ways to do it for less money. For example, if you are paying $200 a week for lawn care and landscaping, that amounts to more than $10,000 annually. But some companies offer a discount if you pay the annual bill up front. If your landscaper offers a 20 percent discount, you save more than $2,000.

Find enough discounts like this, and a church can save a lot of money. This is what we have been doing for years. We shop around and find the best prices, and we take advantage of every special offer or incentive. You can do it too. Do your homework. Opportunities to save money are out there, but you have to look for them. Negotiate wisely. It will make a major impact on your finances, and it will show your members that you are serious about stewardship.

DEALING WITH DEBT

I understand that people will read this book in the aftermath of the coronavirus crisis, so I want to emphasize that reducing expenses is especially critical if your church or organization is struggling with debt. The same goes for personal debt.

If you are struggling with debt, you must do two things: Increase your income and reduce your expenses.

How do you increase income in a church, especially one affected by a national health crisis? First, teach your people how to manage their money. Second, show them that their church is handling its finances wisely. Some churches launch campaigns focused on reducing debt. This might seem like a good idea, but I have learned that people aren't motivated by such campaigns. They don't relate well to them.

On the other hand, most people will gladly give to a ministry effort, even if they don't have much to give. They will sacrifice to feed the poor or provide relief in the wake of a natural disaster. They give because efforts like these are meaningful on a personal and spiritual level. They see their fellow humans suffering, and it touches their hearts. For example, one Sunday, we raised $150,000 via a special offering to support relief efforts after a tsunami. Our people stepped up and gave generously.

But if I had said, "Today I want to collect an offering to pay off three million dollars' worth of debt," people would not have supported that cause. So, instead of focusing on debt reduction, encourage people to give extra money to ministry efforts. Hopefully, this giving will result in budget surpluses among your various ministries. Take those funds and employ them to reduce debt.

Being faithful about attacking debt allowed us to pay off our Ministry Center in just six years. (That payoff also included $10 million in improvements to the building.) We built our $62 million Worship Center and paid off half of the cost before we moved into the building. More recently we built our $23 million Family Life Center, which we didn't need to finance. We had the whole $23 million in the bank. This was a significant achievement for our church, and I encourage you to apply the principles we used, which I'll explain right now.

When we develop our annual budget, we consider the previous year's revenue. For example, if our 2022 revenue is $1 million, for 2023 we would budget to spend ten percent less in expenses than the 2022 revenue. That would mean that our 2023 spending should not exceed $900,000. Let's assume that our 2023 spending matches our budget and our revenue matches 2022's ($1 million). At the end of 2023, we should have at least $100,000 in the bank. By conservatively anticipating that our 2023 revenue will match 2022—and by resolving to avoid spending *all* of that revenue—we enjoy a budget surplus at the end of the year. What's more, our church has established a track record of always bringing in more revenue than the year before. So, if we bring in $1.2 million by the end of 2023, we'll have a $300,000 budget surplus.

Sadly, most churches plan to spend every dime they take in, so they will never learn how to effectively manage money. They go into debt to finance building improvements, they fail to earn interest on their savings (because they have none), and they miss opportunities to save money by paying up front for goods and services.

In most churches, the leaders say, "We're going to believe the Lord for $1.2 million," then they set their annual budget for exactly that amount. They make all kinds of plans for a variety of ministry activities. But when it's time to pay for all those ministries, the funds aren't there.

What happens next? Church leaders pressure the congregation. They beat them up and nag them. And people stop attending, because who wants to hear about their church's money problems every Sunday? Please don't let this happen to you. Focus on reducing expenses and crafting a budget that is leaner than it was the year before.

I realize that cutting back is a challenge, regardless of a church's size or budget. To help us budget frugally, I've trained my staff to create a buffer in the budget, and with the exception of one year, they have met the challenge. On the year in question, I was presented with a budget that called for spending every dime we took in. I asked my staff to try again. I said that we simply weren't going to budget that way. (Imagine the implications for a year of COVID-19 or some other big emergency.) My staff met the challenge. They came back with a revised budget that put the buffer back in.

Of course, you do not have to start with a 10 percent buffer. You can start at 5 percent or wherever you are comfortable. If money is tight at your church, start at 2 percent and work your way up.

When it comes to making budget cuts, don't proclaim that you want to make a 5 percent cut across the board, with every department or ministry being affected equally. Instead, ask "What can we do without?" or "Where can we scale back?" *That's* where you make the cuts.

As noted earlier, I bear ultimate accountability for each budget cut, so I take these decisions seriously. I do my homework. I talk with everyone involved. I get input on who will be affected. I weigh carefully the financial, personal, and ministerial ramifications.

When I'm working with committees, I look for possible alternatives. Could two programs be combined into one? Could a full-time staff position transition to part-time or seasonal, rather than being eliminated? Could we partner with a church in our community to provide a program that neither church can sustain alone?

Here's an example of how our church put budgeting principles into action: We used to give people annual bonuses at Christmas, provided they were performing at an excellent level. However, after witnessing years of every manager reporting that every employee was performing at an excellent (bonus-worthy!) level, I had to make a change.

The Christmas bonuses are gone. Now, if someone wants a raise, it is going to be based on their actual work performance. After all, that's the way it should be. A small Christmas gift might spring from the kindness of someone's heart, but a work-related bonus, regardless of its size, must be *earned*. It's remarkable how wise budgeting and accountability go hand in hand.

I want to encourage you by sharing that we have never compromised on these budgeting principles, and God has shown us his favor for our diligence. I want your church to experience this favor too.

We teach these same financial management principles to our church members. They need to know how to manage their money, so we provide financial-management classes. Additionally, I teach an annual series on finances and money management. A highlight of the series is strategies for getting out of debt and a credit card cutting service. We place a large empty water cooler in front of the altar and provide several pairs of scissors. As I'm teaching, I encourage people who feel convicted about getting out of debt to come forward, cut up their credit cards, and drop the pieces in the container. So many people respond that the container almost overflows with credit card bits.

I present a tithing message every year, featuring an illustration I learned from the late Reverend Dr. Wyatt Tee Walker, a prominent figure in the Civil Rights Movement, as well as a theologian, scholar, and pastor of Canaan Baptist Church of Christ in Harlem, New York. I purchase fifty pieces of fruit: ten oranges; ten apples; ten bananas, and so on. I set up two tables and place forty-five items on one table and five on the other. The first table represents our harvest, the fruit we will consume. The other table is God's; it's the table for tithes to him. The two tables present a clear picture: God will bless you with abundant fruit, 90 percent of everything you harvest. All he asks is that you give 10 percent to him. Dr. Walker's model has proven to be a very effective way to illustrate tithing to my congregation.

I use this illustration every year, even though people have seen it over and over again. Why the repetition? Here's how I see it: If the choir can sing the same song over and over again, the pastor ought to be able to preach the same sermon once in a while. The congregation shouts along with the same song, in the same location, and sung in the same key by the same soloist. It's played by the same musicians on the same instruments— same everything! That's why I preach the same sermon. When I preach that same sermon, an amazing thing happens: Many people get saved during the tithing message! It resonates with people. We teach our people about finances and so much more through repetition and practical, relatable application.

We teach people how to get out of debt, and we encourage them to learn how to manage their money. That's how to avoid more debt later on. We teach them how to pray for money. We teach them how to get the best buy for their dollar. We teach them all of these things every year, through classes and from the pulpit. And every year it makes a huge impact.

The people in your church want to tithe, but because they are so burdened economically, they feel they cannot afford to. If you do not teach them how to get out of debt and stay out of debt—how to manage their money—they will never be able to tithe.

Chapter Eight

Staff for Success

Another critical part of managing the church budget is allocating funding for staffing. Staffing is critical because churches cannot run effectively on volunteers alone. I realize some readers will beg to differ with me on this principle, especially leaders of small churches who might not have any budget for paid support staff or independent contractors or laborers. But I want to share a principle that has worked for us, and I believe it will work for you too: I do not expect volunteers to do everything. I just don't. Some roles are best filled by paid staff or a paid independent contractor.

Of course, all churches rely on some volunteers, so how do you decide whom to pay, especially given a tight budget? Two questions help me decide who should be a paid staff member and who should be a volunteer: If a task or service doesn't get done, what is the impact on the church? How will the undone job reflect on our church and what we are trying to accomplish?

For example, instead of hiring a professional landscaper, you try to save money by recruiting a volunteer to cut and water the grass, eliminate weeds, and manage the church grounds. Then the volunteer decides he's going to take a vacation or go on hiatus. Perhaps he simply stops volunteering because he doesn't have the time or energy anymore. The result? Your grass grows out of control. Weeds pop up everywhere. Trees and bushes become diseased.

How will members feel about their church? And how will potential visitors feel? What about the people who have allergies to all the weeds? This is why I regard landscaping and lawn care as a critical function, something worth paying for. That's why I pay our janitors too.

Here again, some churches try to save money by asking members to tidy up the building after services are complete. But what happens if the members fail to pick up? They return to church the following Sunday, and there is trash everywhere. Think of how this can affect a worship service.

Compensation is important because it makes people accountable. If you are being paid for your work, you understand that your paycheck comes with expectations. You will be held accountable for failing to do your job, and there are probably multiple people eager to step up and collect that paycheck if you're not willing to earn it.

What's more, the Scripture teaches clearly (in Leviticus 25:17 and Luke 6:31, for example) that we should not take advantage of people. And anyone who has been part of a church for any length of time knows that volunteers are taken advantage of, sometimes for years.

So, if you have an ongoing task that is completed regularly

by the same person (or team of people), compensation is warranted. This is a rule I live by.

If you decide to add a paid position to your budget, please avoid a trap that some churches step into. They hire someone and try to match the salary that person was earning in the secular business world. That is an error. The pay for every job needs to be based on your budget and the nature of the work being done for *your church*.

Let's say you want to hire an administrative assistant from a large tech firm in your city. He or she might come with impressive credentials, but your church doesn't have the budget of a tech giant. Your church's job description will look a lot different as well. On a similar note, we pay our janitors based on their specific duties for our church. We don't need to match the custodial pay range of a large hospital or government building.

We currently have almost 400 employees at First Baptist Church of Glenarden. Every job's pay is based on the job description and the skill level of the employee. We have a Human Resources Department that helps us establish pay scales, and we strive to be as fair as possible. But, again, we don't try to match salaries with the mainstream market. Instead, our employees can increase their pay by earning a promotion, learning new skills, or simply becoming more proficient at doing their jobs. I realize that a small church probably can't afford a Human Resources Department to set pay scales. If this is the case for your church, consider partnering with a larger church in your community. They might have a pay scale you can adopt (and adjust). They might have research they would be willing to share with you.

Our church does this all of the time for other churches. We are happy to share our knowledge, research, and experiences with others. It's another way we can ensure that churches cooperate with one another, rather than compete.

I want to conclude this chapter with a few thoughts on volunteers, because they are the unsung heroes of so many churches. But, too often, they aren't treated like heroes. They are taken advantage of, worn down, and overworked. Sometimes they are strung along, with the promise of becoming paid staff members, but that promise is never fulfilled.

Here are a few volunteer guidelines that have worked well for us.

First, on any given Sunday, we ensure that no volunteer works *all* of the services. They need time to simply be a parishioner and be fed spiritually.

Second, we don't ask our volunteers to serve on multiple ministries. This guideline is based on the same principles as the one above. Just as you shouldn't have someone managing the nursery during the early service then overseeing the parking lot during the later service, it's not fair to have one person who serves on the hospitality committee, the missions committee, and provides the ASL interpretation for every worship service.

Finally, set a time limit on volunteer positions. When we enlist a volunteer, we make sure it's for a mutually amenable period of time—usually six months or one year. This helps avoid volunteer burnout, and it can help any church avoid running its volunteers straight into the ground. Further, I believe you will be able to recruit more volunteers if people know they aren't signing the rest of their lives away.

Chapter Nine

Master Marketing, Social Media, and Technology

Every effective leader should understand the importance of reaching the next generation because that generation will lead our churches into the future. Many church congregations die because they fail to understand the importance of reaching and connecting with future leaders.

If you want your church to grow and reach future generations, you must meet them where they are. You have to go where they go. You have to understand and participate in the things that interest them. That's why it's vital that church leaders embrace a variety of marketing, mass media, social media, and technologies as we strive to expand our reach and ministry.

At FBC, our in-person worship services and Bible studies attract about 11,000 people each week. However, an additional 19,000 people tune in online. Technology allows us to more than double our reach, to serve many people who might not be able to participate in our traditional services for various reasons. (In addition to being able to watch our services online, people can listen to an audio-only streaming option or a rebroadcast on two local radio stations.)

I know that many of you reading this book are early adopters when it comes to technology, but I admit that this is an area where it took me a while to grow. It was outside my comfort zone to learn all the ways people communicate and share information today. Then I had to tap into the new technologies and discover how to participate in an authentic way. I come from the generation where we lifted up Jesus by preaching and teaching from the pulpit, and we did not need to do much else to reach people. That worked fine for us, because people were willing to come to the church to get what they needed. However, my generation will not be around in the future, so we must position our churches *now* for future sustainability and growth.

We live in a culture where people learn and get information from a wide array of sources. To reach them, we must go where they are. For example, most people are glued to their smartphones all day long. According to 2021 Pew research, 96 percent of Americans ages eighteen to twenty-nine own a smartphone. The percentage is almost as high (95 percent) ages thirty to forty-nine. The number is lower for those over sixty-five, at 61 percent, but it is significant that well over half of people in this age group are smartphone owners.[3]

Additionally, 2021 research from Statista indicates that 20 percent of Americans ages eighteen to thirty-four spend forty hours or more *each week* on their smartphones. The percentage is almost as high (19 percent) for those ages thirty-five to fifty-four. The percentage drops by more than half (to 9 percent) for Americans over fifty-five, but it would be a mistake to assume modern tech is a tool only for the young. According to Statista, 17 percent of the 55+ demographic spends from ten to nineteen hours a week on a smartphone, and 18 percent spend from five to nine hours.[4]

Today, people of all ages get their information (including local and national news) from social media. They make buying and participation decisions based on websites. They want to access entertainment and education at their convenience, not that of the content provider.

The implications for today's churches are obvious. People want to learn about your church via your website. They want to be able to stream your worship services and special events. They want phone apps that allow them to give tithes and offerings through their preferred payment processor.

In short, we must embrace our culture the way Jesus did in his day—and he embraced everyone, everywhere. Jesus placed no limitations on reaching people and sharing the gospel with them. In Matthew 28:19, he instructs, "Therefore, go and make disciples of all the nations" (NIV). The New Century Version of this verse renders it, "So go and make followers of all people in the world." We need to take that same approach, and if we want our churches to be relevant in the future, we have to do the work *today*. That means showing up outside the four walls of the church by finding effective ways to employ various forms of media and technology.

In Matthew 5:16, Jesus says, "Let your light shine before others, that they may see your good deeds and glorify your Father in heaven" (NIV). Jesus teaches us to let our light shine, so our church, with integrity and great care, employs various forms of marketing, mass media, and social media to reach people.

I encourage you to investigate how you can use modern media to reach out and connect with people. There is much competition for their time and attention, so it's vital that you make your work known. I know that many of you reading this book are doing great things in your churches or other ministries. Unfortunately, a lot of people don't know about those things, because you are not promoting them effectively. So I encourage you to use radio, television, websites, apps, and social media to broaden your reach.

Over the years, our church has grown substantially in this area because we dedicated paid staff to our efforts, and we created ministries that help us spread the word about the work we are doing. We created a Communications Department, which manages all of our internal and external marketing and messaging efforts. Any time we hold events or sponsor major initiatives, our Communications Department makes sure we promote it through radio advertising, local news reporting, email blasts, and the church's website and social media platforms.

We have hired professionals who know how to design innovative marketing campaigns to reach people efficiently and effectively. We have forged relationships with local radio and TV stations to help us share what we are doing in our community and connect people with the ministries we offer.

Our social media ministry helps promote our church's events and initiatives through platforms like Instagram, Facebook, and Twitter. We have created a Facebook community where thousands of people connect and interact every day. They share resources for new members, discuss recent sermon and Bible-study topics, share prayer requests, and engage in lighthearted exchanges about topics they find fun and interesting.

I want to emphasize social media because its impact is huge. Today's youth, in particular, do virtually everything by social media, so you cannot ignore it. We started a new youth ministry in our church, and on the first day, 3,000 people showed up. Where did almost all of them hear about it? Social media.

It's important to note that you can't rely on only one form of social media. It's not one-size-fits-all. People from different age groups and backgrounds favor different flavors of social media.

For example, a 2020 survey revealed that Snapchat is the most important social network for teens (at 34 percent). TikTok is running a close second (favored by 29 percent of today's teens). Facebook isn't even in teens' top five anymore. Only 2 percent of them say it's their most important platform. Ages twenty-five to thirty-five constitute Facebook's largest demographic (at 26 percent). Meanwhile, more than 40 percent of Twitter users are between eighteen and twenty-nine. Conversely, only 7 percent of Americans sixty-five and older use Twitter.[5]

I should note that lots of people use multiple platforms. Social media is constantly evolving, and what people like one day can change the next. Today's church leaders can enhance ministry effectiveness by staying abreast of the trends in social media to ensure they are active on the most relevant platforms.

I've grown considerably in my understanding of social media, but it took a while to get there. I had to ask for help to get comfortable with everything. But now I have active social media accounts that allow me to engage with people all over the world. It's amazing. People ask questions, share testimonies, and get connected with the resources our church has to offer—all through social media.

Media and technology are great ways to get your message out there and spread it to the masses. Without it, you miss an opportunity to reach people who rely heavily on various online platforms for information, entertainment, and influence.

Of course, technology will never take the place of face-to-face human interaction. We church leaders, of all people, should always remember this. Technology can lead people to opportunities for in-person fellowship. In times of crisis (such as a global pandemic), it can serve as a temporary alternative to in-person worship or instruction. But it should never replace the good we can do by being physically present for one another.

I encourage you to be aware of other potential pitfalls of technology as well. First, make sure your online messages are true and accurate. Don't overpromise when it comes to wealth, happiness, a problem-free life, or anything else.

Second, don't over-rely on Twitter, texting, or any other method when it comes to meaningful conversations. Tech can be a great way to start a conversation or tackle a problem, but there is no substitute for a meaningful personal conversation. On a similar note, it's tempting to resort to an online message when it's time to deliver bad news or share a critique. Resist this temptation. If you need to communicate something difficult, be willing to be fully present.

Third, don't use social media or anything else to compete with other churches or criticize other ministries. At FBC, we strive to encourage people and share what we have to offer our community. The focus is on what we are trying to do for people, not on what others are *not* doing, or not doing well.

Finally, remember that the internet is forever. We all need to be careful about posting an angry message in haste, accidentally sharing confidential information, or jumping the gun on time-sensitive information. Yes, we can delete a post from our Facebook page or remove a story from our website, but it might have been shared hundreds or even thousands of times before then.

Like it or not, in today's world many people will judge your church by your online presence, just as they do with other businesses or organizations. If I moved to your community and heard about your church, I would check you out online. If your website was outdated and unprofessional (or if you had *no* website), I wouldn't even visit your church. A church without an up-to-date and visually compelling website is at least twenty years behind the times. You will repel anyone looking for a church that embraces contemporary culture.

It's worth repeating: You must have an effective website. And you must be capable of communicating across a spectrum of media.

TECHNOLOGY OF THE TIMES

Technology goes hand-in-hand with new media and social media, and your church should reflect this. Use video screens, computer labs, phone systems, video editing systems, and more. In short, be open to using technology when and where you can do it effectively, wisely, and with honesty and integrity. Technology is not a cure-all, as we saw in the previous section, and it will never replace the importance of face-to-face interaction and connection. But it can be an excellent way to help you get the word out about your ministry.

I realize that cost is a concern, especially for smaller churches, but the prices of equipment and various systems have dipped significantly in recent years. I worked in television before becoming a full-time pastor, and back in the day, a high-quality camera could cost $200,000 to $300,000. But not anymore. As many of us learned after the pandemic, a variety of high-def video cameras are available for under a thousand dollars.

Consider updating the systems you use to help people participate in and support your various ministries. I already discussed online giving, but I want to note here that it's vital to use technology to modernize the way your church receives tithes and offerings.

Today, most people do all their banking and bill paying online. Imagine being one of these completely paperless people and receiving a packet of offering envelopes in the mail with instructions to put cash or a check inside and bring them to church each week!

With each passing day, more people consider it archaic

and inconvenient for a church to lack online payment options. Many of today's consumers never carry cash and don't even own a checkbook anymore. I confess that I once hesitated to embrace online giving. However, now that we have invested in the technology needed to provide multiple online giving options, we are seeing most of our revenue coming through these platforms.

I realize that some pastors worry about potential pitfalls of these technologies. For example, does someone's use of an autopay app remove the intentionality associated with regular tithing? Will they lose the opportunity to reflect on God's provision for their lives, as well as the good their tithe might accomplish?

We have not found this to be the case. First, the decision to commit to regular and automatic contributions to the church is, in itself, an act of intentionality and worship. It's a way of saying, "I'm all in. This money is going to my church regularly. I'm removing the temptation to skip a month or decrease my contribution." Further, automated giving doesn't rob anyone of the opportunity to reflect, meditate, or pray about the act of giving. For example, if you schedule your autopay contribution for the first of the month, you can set aside time for reflection on that day. You can even use technology to remind you about that time of reflection and prayer.

Technology has drastically lightened the administrative burden of counting checks and cash—and dealing with the fees and headaches associated with bounced checks. Such problems are minimal now. Watching the new systems work has helped me understand the importance of embracing the technologies that reflect the way people live today. If your church allows people to use technology the way they do in their everyday lives, they will appreciate it and gladly participate.

Another area where we have expanded our technology is in our activity-registration and membership-tracking systems. Years ago, people filled our hallway, waiting in line after church to register for classes, conferences, and ministry events. We recorded each person's information on paper and took their payments via cash or check. Then, of course, someone had to process all that paperwork, deposit the cash and checks via the Finance Office, create and update rosters of everyone who registered, and on, and on, and on.

Imagine doing this for thousands of people—because that is what we did. We saw people tire of waiting in long lines and simply give up without registering for a class or conference they truly wanted to attend. (If only we hadn't made it so difficult.) Others would persevere, finally arriving at the front of a line, only to find that the class they wanted was full.

And then there were the inevitable clerical errors: Paperwork got lost. Names were accidentally omitted from class lists. People were placed in the wrong class. And drama ensued.

I should note that such errors can happen in churches of all sizes. Even a small church can benefit from more reliable and efficient systems. For example, I know of small churches where all of the Sunday school or Bible-study information is stored in the mind or handwritten in the notebook of one person. But what happens if this person has a health crisis or leaves the church abruptly? We can all appreciate the difference between accessing needed information from clearly marked and diligently updated computer files and the guess-work and frustration of solving a mystery with virtually no clues.

At FBC, it became clear that our outdated methods were not only time consuming but also inefficient and prone to error, so we invested in online systems that streamlined our processes. Now people do not have to wait in line to regis-ter for classes, conferences, or ministry events. They can do everything online, including making payments, either through our website or a third-party registration system.

We can automatically run reports to generate attendee rosters, which reveal exactly who has registered and paid. We also track class attendance so we know which classes people have taken and whether they have met their course attendance requirements. This is particularly important because certain classes are required for anyone wanting to serve as a teacher or leader in our church.

By implementing technology in our registration systems, we now have classes that are filled to capacity because we have made it easy for people to register. And when courses fill up, people can easily peruse the online course catalog to see what else is available.

What's more, our ministry events sell out—without all kinds of drama and desperation—because we have made it easy to purchase tickets. We are much more efficient in the way we staff and operate our major volunteer events, like our annual Thanksgiving Basket Giveaway, which allows us to serve several thousand people without being overstaffed or understaffed.

Our current systems allow us to manage volunteer registrations online, and we can easily communicate instructions and assignments to our volunteers. This helps us serve our community with excellence, which in turn, draws more people to our ministry.

Implementing technological advances has made our church more efficient across the board. It's so much easier for people to participate in our activities and ministries. I've learned that if people are inconvenienced for too long, they will get frustrated and move on to something that is more convenient. So we are always looking for ways to use technology to make things easier for people. That way, they will be excited about taking advantage of everything available to them.

Because there is so much competition for everyone's time and attention, expanding your reach and embracing technology are more important than ever. That's why I encourage you to use technology and media to maximize your efforts. To reach people today, you must go where they are, and they are all over new media. They use it every day. You should too. After all, much of the content on social media is unhealthy. We need more positive voices on social media. We need to both monitor and combat how social media is harming people mentally, emotionally, and physically. Today's church has the opportunity to use social media for good. My fellow pastors, let's avoid Twitter battles with parishioners, other pastors, and internet trolls. These distract us from our primary ministry duties and our families. Such battles can also make us argumentative and angry too much of the time.

Let's not get trapped in online feedback loops that cut us

off from alternative viewpoints and skew our perspective of what our congregations and our communities truly think and feel. Let's use social media, and technology in general, to tell everyone what our ministries can do for them and how we can help them impact their world.

Part Three

Build Up
God's People

Chapter Ten

Value the Art of Evangelism

Ask the leader of almost any church if evangelism is important, and you will receive a predictable answer: "Of course it is." However, many church leaders have no plan or strategy to make their churches evangelistic. Not surprisingly, there's rarely any effort either.

According to 2021 Statista research, only 22 percent of American adults attend church regularly. This is a significant drop; in 2009, almost half of Americans attended church regularly. Meanwhile, 31 percent of Americans *never* attend. Further, Barna Research Group (in its State of the Church 2020 research) revealed that one in three *practicing* Christians have stopped attending the church they attended before COVID-19.[6]

The numbers are even more depressing among the younger

generations (whom we will discuss in detail in a later chapter). For example, nearly two-thirds of Americans between eighteen and twenty-nine have ended their church involvement after being active as children and/or teens. What does all of this mean? Your church members, more than ever, have relatives, coworkers, friends, and neighbors who do not participate in church. In fact, recent Gallup research has revealed that in 2020—for the first time in more than eight decades—the number of Americans who *did not* attend church surpassed the number of those who did.[7]

This is disturbing information. After all, if our church members follow Jesus and have a faith that is deeply meaningful to them, that should inspire the people around them to have a thirst for Christ. We hope that as people interact with our church members, they will be inspired to live lives of meaning, service, and love for God.

SHEEP MAKE SHEEP

At First Baptist, we are grateful and humbled that we are bucking the trends. Every week, we see about a hundred people make a decision for Christ, and our ministries for teens and young adults continue to thrive. We wouldn't have numbers like this unless our church consistently drew hundreds of guests.

During our worship services, we ask guests or visitors to stand. I do this for two reasons. First, I want to welcome these people. Second, the number of people who stand each week helps me gauge the health and vitality of our church. If our people's spiritual lives are healthy and dynamic, their relatives, friends, and coworkers will want to discover what made the difference.

If, for example, "Don" is not the person he used to be because something dynamic has happened in his life, his friends and family members will be curious. They will wonder, "Why is Don suddenly so joyful all of the time?"

That's why we have hundreds of people visiting our church every week.

But if I looked over the sanctuary one Sunday and saw no guests, I would know the sheep were sick. That would concern me because it is not solely the pastor's job to make the church grow. Sheep make more sheep.

That is how our church has grown—by sheep making sheep. We did not build our church by bringing in a lot of big-name speakers or famous gospel singers. Yes, we occasionally invite well-known artists and speakers, but we did not build the church that way. We built our church through the members going out and talking to their friends, relatives, coworkers, and neighbors. They shared the gospel with such excitement that people came to our church and accepted Christ. We taught our sheep how to make more sheep, and they took it from there.

It is not solely the pastor's job to make the church grow. Sheep make more sheep.

Over time, our process for teaching our members how to share the gospel has evolved. Before I became the pastor, First Baptist was a traditional Baptist church. If people came forward to become members of the church, the leaders would direct them to a back room, collect their contact information, and then return them to the sanctuary. Then everyone waited for someone to make a motion in favor of accepting the prospective members. Next, the congregation voted on the motion. (Yes, sinners voted on whether other sinners could be a part of our church.) That was the tradition at that time.

When I became the pastor, I changed that process. Today, if people come forward, I don't direct them to a back room where deacons ask for names, addresses, and phone numbers. Instead, we clear the front row and invite the prospective members to have a seat.

Then, with the congregation as a witness, I walk people through the Romans Road to Salvation, a set of verses from the book of Romans that lead to a saving knowledge of Jesus. (Those Scriptures are Romans 3:10; 3:23; 5:12; 6:23a; 5:8; 6:23b; 10:9–10; 10:13.) After about six months of this process, everyone in the church knew the Romans Road to Salvation.

I used this approach because I wanted every church member to know the Romans Road so they could confidently lead others to Christ.

I don't do that on Sundays anymore, because we now have a Romans Road class, specifically designed to help people share the gospel. That class fills up quickly every time we offer it.

It's worth noting that the other perennial favorite class is our Financial Freedom series. This tells me a lot about our membership and their needs.

Teaching our members how to share the gospel has been huge for us. Our training emphasizes that people do not have to get saved at church. They can get saved at their jobs, in their neighborhoods, at the gym—anywhere.

We teach our members, "You can lead people to the Lord anywhere, and *then* bring them to church." As a result, people join our church regularly, many saying things like, "I got saved at my job by Sister Leslie." Then we celebrate Sister Leslie, as we do everyone who wins people to the Lord and encourages others to do likewise. In fact, our primary method of church growth is our members, who bring in their friends, relatives, and coworkers.

IT'S ALL ABOUT RELATIONSHIPS

I have six children, and when my youngest daughter was in high school, she played on the basketball team even though she hates sports. You might be wondering why. I wondered too.

Here's how my daughter's athletic career began: One day she came home and told me she was on the soccer team. So I started attending her games. And do you know what I saw? She never touched the ball! She just ran up and down the field.

I didn't understand what was going on, so I asked her, "You don't like sports. You don't watch them on television. You don't know who the star athletes are. Why are you running up and down the field, but not actually kicking the ball? Why do you get mad if we're late driving you to practice?"

Her answer was simple. It was all about her friends. Her friends were on the soccer team, and she wanted to be with them. It was the same thing with basketball a few years later.

Yes, my daughter spent hours every week doing something she *disliked*. And this continued for years, all because of her relationships with her friends.

This is an important lesson for all of us ministry leaders: Many people join a church and stay connected because of *relationships*. That's why we teach our members how to develop relationships and create relationship-based opportunities to share the gospel with the people in their lives.

What does this mean for you? You must have a *strategy* for evangelism. Evangelism doesn't happen on its own. You need to create a strategy and implement it, just as you would for any other aspect of your church. If your church lacks an evangelism strategy, it's not going to grow.

We also have a process of certifying people to be altar counselors. That way, when someone joins our church, we immediately pair him or her with an altar counselor—someone to partner with them, hug them, and learn where they are spiritually. Our counselors minister to people based on their specific spiritual condition.

> Evangelism doesn't happen on its own. You need to create a strategy and implement it.

If someone is backslidden, for example, his counselor will walk him through the process of rededicating his life to Christ.

If someone is not saved, the counselor will walk her to Jesus, via the aforementioned Romans Road.

For those unsure about their salvation status, counselors will lead them through the Scriptures so they can be sure.

If someone says, "I am already saved, and I want to be a member of your church," a counselor will ensure that there has been a genuine born-again regeneration experience.

Ultimately, our church is growing because sheep are

sharing the gospel. I encourage and challenge churches to train people to be evangelistic in their conversations. Build a culture of evangelism, starting with your church leaders. Expect those leaders to make evangelism part of their everyday lives. Why? Because members adopt the heart of the church leaders.

If your leaders don't cultivate and demonstrate a lifestyle of evangelism, your members won't either. Teach leaders and members how to engage in spiritual conversations with unspiritual people. It will help your church grow because that's what it is doing for ours.

Chapter Eleven

Discern the Way
to Worship

I pray that you are noticing some major themes in this book. One of these themes is that a church must embrace and respond to contemporary culture if it wants to grow.

I want to be clear: I am not suggesting that we compromise on preaching and teaching biblical truths. I believe the church should *not* conform to cultural norms that are not based on God's Word. For example, tolerance is a cultural norm, and embracing tolerance can help people respect the rights, backgrounds, and personal beliefs of others. However, there are things the church cannot tolerate, such as dishonesty or immoral behavior.

However, I recommend that our churches strive to understand today's culture and embrace people where they are so we can reach them and draw them to Christ. That's why it's important to evaluate the way we do church. After all, some of us have been doing church the same way for a hundred years, and many people are simply not responding.

In the next few pages, I'll explain why people are not responding. I'll suggest the need to evaluate our worship services and make other adjustments to ensure that our churches are positioned for impact and growth.

THE NEED FOR BIBLICAL PRINCIPLES

I imagine that some of you are wondering why your church isn't attracting new members or retaining current members. Here's one possible reason: Few people are drawn to a church that fails to provide clear, biblically based preaching and teaching. And even fewer will stick with a church that fails to deliver practical content rooted in the wisdom of God's Word.

I've visited churches and seen the pastor open his Bible and share a Scripture reading. Then he closes the Bible and doesn't mention that Scripture for the rest of the sermon. That's a problem because people need to hear more than the pastor's ideas or philosophies. They need to hear a word from the Lord. That is why we have built our church on biblically based preaching and teaching that minister to people's *practical* needs.

I highlighted the word practical for a good reason. You see, I could talk about Moses and how he stretched out his rod and parted the Red Sea. "Ain't God all right?" I could ask. "Won't he do miracles for you?" But if that's all I say, the congregation will ask themselves, "How does that apply to my everyday life? What does that mean for me, as I deal with my kids, who are giving me hell right now?"

We must preach and teach biblical principles because that is what people need for their lives. They need to understand what the Bible says about the issues they face every day: anger, forgiveness, finances, marriage, raising children, conflict resolution, morality, and much more. These are the things we talk about at our church. We give people the practical, Bible-based strategies they need so they can deal with their issues and become victorious in those areas of their lives.

SHOUT, BUT SHOUT QUICKLY!

Here's another reason many people don't attend church: There are rituals that carry little or no relevance for the modern person's worship needs.

In the past we have provided up to five Sunday worship services. That means the services must start and finish on time. Let me drop this in your spirit: American culture has changed. Long worship services are no longer practical. Many people work on weekends or have other obligations they have to fulfill. Like it or not, our lives are busy and heavily scheduled. People are seeking efficiency and wise use of time in all areas of their lives, and that includes church. People won't be regulars at your church if your services regularly go into overtime. If you want your church to grow, you must say goodbye to those two-hour-plus services.

We live in a microwave culture, not a slow-cooker culture. So we must adapt. You can keep running Sunday services for two-and-a-half hours if you want, but the sinners won't show up—neither will many of the saints.

So, what does a microwave-culture church service look like? I suggest looking for every opportunity to streamline. We found certain activities that took too much time and made our services unnecessarily long.

For example, various members handled the reading of the Scripture. Often, the reader was sitting in the back of the sanctuary. So we all waited while he or she stood up, maneuvered to the aisle, and walked to the front. Then, of course, he had to find the passage before beginning to read. Those of you who are veteran pastors know that some church members have mobility challenges, and others might struggle to find the right page, especially if they are nervous. We knew this was an area that needed streamlining. Today, if the Scripture reader is on the program, he or she knows to sit up front and have the Bible open to the Scripture ahead of time. Being prepared saves time.

> **You can keep running Sunday services for two-and-a-half hours if you want, but the sinners won't show up—neither will many of the saints.**

Additionally, we used to have folks march around to give their offerings. That took twenty minutes. And I use the word *march* intentionally. Folks didn't merely walk. They had to march. Meanwhile, the rest of us all sat around and waited. So we ended the marching. It simply took too long.

Now we pass offering baskets. *Every* row has a basket. The ushers take the baskets and pass one down each row. Then the ushers collect the baskets, and that's that. The process is consistently completed in two minutes! That's an eighteen-minute difference.

I realize that some of you might believe the old myth that if people march around for offering, they will give more. That is what the old preachers told me, but it's not true! People do what they are taught. If you teach them properly, they will do what they are supposed to do. We stopped marching, and we started taking in *more* money, not less.

I want to note that streamlining the worship service was not the only reason we stopped marching. I stopped the marching because some sisters in the service were not always holy and sanctified in their choice of attire. And when I saw the brothers walking around for offering, not putting anything in the offering plate, but just walking around and looking at the sisters who dressed in a revealing manner, I knew I needed to make a change. Some of you need to make that change too. An abundance of fanfare, in its various forms, is usually not conducive to an efficient and worshipful church experience.

I realize that many church members are accustomed to various traditions and patterns. However, we knew we couldn't offer multiple services unless each had a time limit. To do that, some things had to be cut. For example, we couldn't provide a Scripture reading *and* a responsive reading. And we couldn't let the choir sing for fifteen minutes, no matter how good they sound. We couldn't let people shout for thirty minutes during each service.

Today, I tell my congregation, "You can shout, but shout quickly! Go ahead and get that dance in real quick! And if you really want to dance longer, come to our latest service, because we do not have another service immediately afterward!"

The congregation laughs when they hear this, but they do shout and dance *quickly*!

These are a few examples of our efforts to adapt our ministry to today's culture. We continue to evaluate our practices and ask ourselves what is still relevant and what is not.

TITHING AND ONLINE GIVING

Another way to streamline the offering is to provide online giving options. We have experienced tremendous success with our online giving. As I shared earlier, I was initially reluctant about online giving. I was concerned that if I put a button for online giving on the church website, people would say, "There he goes; he only wants money."

So I put a *tiny* button at the bottom of our home page. You had to scroll down and look carefully to see it. I did not want it to be obvious or intimidating. But do you know what happened? Within about three months, we were getting substantially more per month in online giving. Only then did I move the button from the bottom of the page up to a more prominent spot.

One of the benefits of online giving is that people can use it 24/7. They can give any time. First Baptist also has its own smartphone app, so donors do not have to be at a computer to give. The result? The vast majority of our members now give their tithes and offerings online. We adapted to the way people pay for things, and they have responded.

I've been to churches where the appeal for the offering is excessively long, which often hinders giving rather than encouraging it. Let's face facts: Today's church attendees are not going to be moved to tithe by your twenty-minute lecture during the worship service. Most likely, they have made their decision before entering your doors. That means pastors must stop spending time browbeating people with Scriptures on giving. That won't put another dime in your congregation's pockets or entice them to give more.

We encourage people to give by teaching them consistently. Don't depend on a sales pitch one Sunday. Teach people about giving in the classes you offer. I don't speak before we collect our Sunday offerings. Instead, a presiding minister announces that it's time for the offering. The congregation shouts, and then they give. And that's it.

> **The vast majority of our members now give their tithes and offerings online.**

We have taught our people how and why to give, and we have removed the old rituals. We have taught them money-management principles. As a result, our giving has increased.

AN INVITING INVITATION

Throughout this chapter, I have recommended streamlining your worship services. However, there is one area that deserves plenty of time: the invitation to follow Christ (also known as the invitation to discipleship). I encourage churches to invite people to make commitments to Christ, not merely to join the church. That is the true purpose of the invitation—encouraging people to commit to the Lord—and I cannot stress enough how important that is. Regularly invite people to meet the Lord and get right with him.

Extending your invitation a little will encourage more people to respond. Why? Because as you speak, there are always a few people out there who struggle to come forward. They might need a bit more time to work through the decision-making process. I believe the Holy Spirit is moving in their hearts.

Throughout the invitation, I appeal to the congregation as individuals, addressing them as directly and personally as possible. My goal is for each person to feel *the Holy Spirit is speaking to them.* I don't push church membership; I push a personal walk with God. I ask, "If you die in your present state, where are you going to spend eternity? Are you right with God? Are you confident that you have a right relationship with him?" That is the appeal I make, and people respond.

My appeal focuses on four spiritual conditions, which I will detail below. Once people respond to the invitation, an altar counselor walks them through the Scriptures based on their spiritual condition.

I start the invitation by appealing to individuals who are unsaved and have never accepted Jesus as Lord and Savior. We walk them through each of the Roman's Road passages and lead them through a prayer of salvation (or sinner's prayer). By the end of the counseling session, each person has said and done everything necessary to be saved.

Next, I appeal to individuals who are already saved but are

living in a backslidden state, meaning they are not in a close, consistent fellowship with the Lord, or are living a sinful lifestyle but want to rededicate their lives to Christ. The Scripture references we use here are 1 John 1:9 and Proverbs 28:13.

Third, I appeal to those who are unsure about their salvation and seeking clarity and assurance. We share 1 John 5:13; 3:14; and 3:18–19 to provide them assurance of their salvation.

After appealing to the first three spiritual conditions, I address people who are already saved but need a church home. We use Hebrews 13:7 and Hebrews 13:17 to underscore that the Lord wants them to be connected with a church. If they have never been baptized, we encourage them to be baptized according to the Scriptures (specifically Matthew 28:19–20; Mark 16:16; and Acts 2:41).

It's vital for today's church to take the time to invite people to make a decision to follow Christ. However, that invitation must be relevant and relatable. This chapter has provided ways to streamline a worship service, but as I said at the beginning of this section, the invitation deserves time. Don't belabor things unnecessarily, but invest the minutes you need to appeal to people's hearts and minds and invite them to follow Jesus.

Chapter Twelve

Understand and Teach Discipleship

In this chapter, I will delve deeper into the importance of discipleship and why we have made it the driving force behind the vision and mission of our church. Of all the principles I share in this book, discipleship—the process of teaching people biblical principles, modeling how to follow Jesus, and spreading the gospel—is the most important.

Discipleship is so important that I want you to put a big star next to this chapter's title. Here's what our church is about: discipleship, discipleship, and discipleship. Why? Because Jesus commands us to be disciples who make new disciples. Discipleship is a way of life.

However, I know of many churches who do everything *but* discipleship. They hold concerts and rallies. They raise money. But they don't disciple people, as Jesus commands us to do. If you are not discipling people, change or shut down! Discipling is what we are called to do. Every church should be striving to help people become like Jesus, look like Jesus, act like Jesus, and talk like Jesus.

OUR DISCIPLESHIP PROCESS

At First Baptist, we have built a foundation on teaching people to be like Jesus. Developing disciples is our priority. We provide classes that focus on Jesus's teachings—for couples, men, women, singles, children, and young adults. We consistently strive to develop disciples at all levels. What's more, we provide classes that apply God's principles to every area of life—from finances to family to the job front. I believe that this focus is one reason God has smiled on us and shown his favor to our church.

> **If you are not discipling people, change or shut down!**

We develop our leaders to be like Jesus so they can influence *others* to be like him—by pouring into them what they have learned. We have created a variety of venues for building disciples and provide many opportunities for all our people to be discipled. You must provide a variety of settings to serve a variety of people and their unique needs.

For example, we offer a three-year men's discipleship program. (Yes, three *years*, not three months.) It's a serious commitment, but we use this program to prepare men for church leadership. We target specific men and invite them to sign on. This invitation-only program has produced many leaders in our church, and it continues to work for us.

The men meet every Saturday morning as they work through the three-year curriculum. The first year focuses on learning discipleship principles. During the second year, the focus shifts to applying those principles to everyday life. The men are held accountable, evaluated, and challenged by their fellow students and by the program leader. During the third year, the men work on pouring all they have learned and experienced into the lives of other people.

Of course, not all our programs run for three years. Our goal is to offer a variety of opportunities so we can meet everyone's discipleship needs.

We start the discipleship process as soon as people respond to the invitation, which I described in the previous chapter. When it comes to discipleship, we don't wait. We start right away so people get connected immediately and move in the direction of discipleship.

When a person joins our church, they are required to complete our class for new members. Next comes our class on foundational principles. This class was designed for newly saved, but we encourage new church members to participate as well. This class, based on Hebrews 6, explains the foundations of the Christian faith.

We recently launched a new discipleship initiative called Life Groups. This initiative marks a significant transition to small cell groups. Facilitators are vetted and trained to lead small group meetings in their homes.

The facilitators invite people they know, with a focus on those who don't attend church or who attend but don't participate in any ministries. In these small groups, the facilitator leads discussions on each week's sermon or Bible-study topic.

The goal here is to broaden our approach to discipleship and share the gospel with people who have little or no connection with a church. Life Groups are vital, because we must face the reality that many people simply don't attend church anymore. Thus, they are not getting discipled. We have found that a small group setting is an effective way to reach these people and draw them to the Lord.

If you do not have a strategy for connecting people to your church, you will miss the opportunity to start discipling them. If people can't make some kind of meaningful connection with your church, they won't attend. Or they might come once or twice, but not return.

Also, I know that some people keep coming to the altar time after time. This is because they never truly connect with anyone at the church and have never been discipled. As I said earlier, sheep make sheep. Disciples make *more* disciples.

Focus on making disciples and watch your ministry grow.

TEACHING DISCIPLESHIP

After someone gives their life to Christ, the most important question is, "What happens next?" People wonder how to follow through on the decision they have just made. They don't want to revert to their former life, but they often have no idea how to start following Jesus and making positive life changes. That's why it is so important to give people the resources and support they need so they can be nurtured as they grow in their Christian walk.

For example, the church must teach people to *practically* apply God's Word to their daily lives. When people speak with me about the sermons that have truly changed their lives, they invariably bring up my most practical sermons—the ones that were easy for them to understand and apply. People will become more like Jesus when they learn about him in a practical way. At our church, we like to address questions like these:

How did Jesus handle criticism?
How did Jesus resolve conflict among the people in
    his life?
What are Jesus's principles for managing money and
    material possessions?
What is Jesus's definition of a good leader?

Most people don't care about understanding Greek and Hebrew. They want to relate personally to Jesus and learn how to emulate him. I know our people will grow if we offer practical training that teaches them how to live effectively.

That's why it's vital that churches clearly teach the Word of God. Every church should provide a weekly Bible study. When I lead a Bible study, that's my opportunity to pour into our people the vision for the church. I talk about our church's goals and the direction we are headed. If I see issues bubbling up in the church, I can address those too. Whatever your church is trying to accomplish, nobody has more influence than the pastor. That's why I take advantage of my opportunities to explain and apply God's Word.

Another way we educate our members is through Bible Institute classes. Our Bible Institute is like a college, in that people can follow specific learning tracks. If you feel a call to the ministry, you can take courses to prepare you for that. If you want to be a counselor, you can jump on that track.

For each ministry role someone wants to pursue, we provide specific prerequisite classes. If you want to be a minister, teacher, or leader in our church, you follow the Leadership Institute track, which includes required classes for each specific role. If someone wants to teach Sunday school, he or she must fulfill all of the requirements before being elevated to that position.

We make sure we equip our various leaders with the skills, knowledge, and experience needed to effectively proclaim the gospel of Jesus Christ and answer the call to ministry. Our ministerial preparation curriculum includes ministers' class, homiletics, expository preaching, how to share the gospel, how to study the Bible, biblical interpretation, and church doctrine. These required courses equip prospective ministers to evangelize, study the Bible, teach, and preach. Additionally, the classes give them a solid understanding of our church's doctrine.

Our Bible Institute classes are not official college courses, but they are modeled on college curricula, and our students do graduate from the Bible Institute. Structuring the Institute this way has encouraged people to commit fully to their course of study. When they graduate, they have something to show for all of their effort. And like at a college or university, people can continue to a higher level of courses, if they so desire.

Our church is not only a place of development for leaders; it's also a place of development for everyone's spiritual walk with God.

When I first became the pastor at FBC, our church offered traditional Bible overview classes, taught by whomever. They were good classes (survey of the Old Testament, survey of the New Testament, and more), but they weren't scratching where people were itching. Spiritual needs were not being met.

Please understand, I think Bible survey classes are great, but many people in today's church are struggling in their marriages, struggling with their kids, and they need help with their finances. They need *practical* classes. A survey of the Pauline epistles is not going to address their deep personal challenges. Once they get the help they urgently need, they will be more interested in a biblical survey course.

Classes that address people's felt needs fill up almost immediately. Here are a few of our most popular offerings:

- FINANCIAL FREEDOM teaches individuals how to manage their money.
- MASTERING MONEY IN YOUR MARRIAGE follows the same curriculum but addresses the unique needs of couples.
- HOMEBUILDERS FOR MARRIAGE focuses on building strong husband/wife relationships.
- DIVORCE CARE ministers to individuals who have experienced divorce or separation.
- HOW TO SHARE THE GOSPEL teaches people how to lead others to Christ. (It's a requirement for our Altar Counselor Certification program.)

- GIFTS OF THE HOLY SPIRIT helps people discover their
  spiritual gifts and how to use them to accomplish
  God's work.

I want to highlight that last class on the list, because today's churches need to do a better job of explaining spiritual gifts. If you are assuming your people know what their spiritual gifts are, I encourage you to rethink that. Many people have no idea what their spiritual gifts are. Others *think* they know, but often cite the gifts they would *like* to have rather than their actual gifting. Too many churches fail to offer classes on spiritual gifts. If your church is one of these, please reconsider. Your members need it.

I know starting a class or program on spiritual gifts can be intimidating, but find a starting point and build from there. First, I committed to learning about spiritual gifts for myself, then I used the knowledge I had gained as the foundation of our spiritual gifts classes. This simple process got us started on a strong foundation. Since then, we have taught so many people and empowered them to use their spiritual gifts. We have helped them understand the role their gifts play in daily life and how they can use their gifts to help others grow and develop as followers of Jesus.

When I became pastor at First Baptist, I taught many of the classes myself. However, I always enlisted an assistant teacher with the goal of having him or her take over the class eventually. This type of mentoring is vital, especially for smaller churches. Every class leader should be developing a future leader. After all, some leaders need a break or a new challenge. Others move away. That's why training someone who can take over is a critical part of building a strong and sustainable educational system.

Over time, I saw a need to enhance our core spiritual gifts classes. I wanted to broaden people's perspectives and help them gain a deeper understanding of their gifts. I realized that such enhancements would require us to train the trainers, so I brought in some wise and experienced leaders to help me. As a result, we are teaching our congregation about spiritual gifts in new ways. Sometimes you have to depart from tradition in order to grow. As a result, we have members who truly understand their own spiritual gifts, and they recognize the gifts of others.

> **Every class leader should be developing a future leader.**

Our members can now relate better, connect more deeply, and minister more effectively to one another.

CHRISTIAN EDUCATION

Our church's Christian Education Department focuses on helping people be more like Jesus. This is one of First Baptist's largest departments. However, you don't need scores of people or huge financial resources to have an effective Christian Education program at your church.

Regardless of how small your church is, start where you are and build over time. If you are the senior pastor (or only pastor) and lack the time or expertise to teach a class, invite someone who can do the job. And if you have the time but not the expertise, find someone to teach you what you need to know. Also consider sending a few potential teachers to nearby churches or organizations to get the training they need. Then they can bring that knowledge back to your church to teach and to train others.

All churches need an educational system. Learn which classes your members need and find a way to meet those needs. I hope one of the methods above will work for you.

Chapter Thirteen

Develop Leadership and Build Character

When I meet people, I always ask, "Where do you attend church?"

One day, I was driving my daughter and two of her friends to the airport. As we talked, I asked the young ladies where they attended church. One told me the name of her church. The other one said she used to attend church but stopped after some drama surrounding the pastor's bad conduct. I was saddened to hear this but not surprised. I have heard this story many times.

If you want to stunt your church's growth, tolerating bad character or poor leadership is a surefire method. Many churches today are seeing drops in attendance and member involvement. Lots of people are turning away from the church, and a lack of character among the leadership is a primary reason. People want to connect with a leader of good character. While some ministries still see success based merely on the leader's charisma and popularity, the well-documented moral failures of so many high-profile church leaders in recent years are changing that story. These days, people are more skeptical of celebrity without character.

If you want to stunt your church's growth, tolerating bad character or poor leadership is a surefire method.

Indeed, bad character and bad leadership are turning away scores of people. John Maxwell notes, "Our character represents who we are on the inside."[8] I agree. Character is who we are when no one is looking. Character is revealed in challenging, high-pressure situations or when difficult decisions must be made. Character dictates how we treat other people. It shows up in the way we carry out our duties and assignments.

Unfortunately for my daughter's friend—and for many people in churches today—a pastor's bad character creates conflict, embarrassment, and deception. Ultimately, it drives people away.

As I work with various churches to help them resolve conflict, I see a familiar pattern. Churches face drama and strife because their pastors have exhibited a lack of character, a deficiency that eventually undermines their effectiveness as leaders. This crisis of character can divide or even destroy a church. But here's the good news: Character and leadership are qualities that can be nurtured and developed. Those of us who are leaders (in church, at home, in the community, in business) need to focus on developing character and leadership in ourselves and in others.

Let's explore how you can create a church environment that allows God to grow character and leadership.

DEVELOPING CHARACTER

God loves positive character, and he is intent on developing his character in each of us. It is an important part of God's program. Earlier in this book, I discussed the importance of building relationships in the context of fulfilling your assignment and advancing the kingdom. God uses relationships to advance his kingdom, of course, but he also uses them to build our character. Romans 8:29 says that God wants us to be conformed to the image of his Son, and that is what character development is all about. What some people fail to appreciate is how much our relationships with others also help us conform to Jesus's image.

> **A pastor's bad character creates conflict, embarrassment, and deception. Ultimately, it drives people away.**

Unfortunately, contemporary culture values and celebrates talent over character. But if we truly want to pursue God's will, we need more than talent. God's heart is not moved by our talent but by our character. *That's* what we need to develop.

For nearly twenty years, our church has focused on developing character in our members, our children, and our staff.

We use a resource called Character First, a leadership train-ing program designed for everyone—children, families, and businesses—to help people learn and live positive values. We do not evaluate the staff only on skill and performance. Character is a key element of every performance review. We rate someone's character by answering questions like these:

"How hospitable is this person?"

"Does he tell the truth?"

"Does he follow through on his responsibilities?"

"Does she demonstrate initiative?"

We regularly take steps to promote positive charac-ter traits and behavior. At our monthly staff meeting, we focus on a specific character trait. We give awards—usually monetary—to staff members who have demonstrated and modeled a trait we have taught. The staff performs skits, pre-pares quizzes, and uses other creative methods to highlight and remind everyone about each character trait. If a staff member has not demonstrated proper character, he or she is counseled about it and challenged to improve.

We train and celebrate strong character among our staff, and we do the same thing with our volunteers. We identify volunteers who demonstrate excellent character traits and reward them with gifts. This helps our volunteers realize what is expected of them.

We also emphasize character development with the chil-dren in our school. We have incorporated the Character First training into the school curriculum. During our monthly Children and Youth service, we acknowledge a young person who has demonstrated good character. We honor children in front of the congregation so everyone can celebrate.

Our core values—including humility, excellence, and honor—are based on good character. I strongly believe that many of our challenges in life are God's way of building and developing our character. The quicker we learn what He wants us to learn, the quicker we can decrease stress and deal with our challenges effectively.

THE PRINCIPLE OF HONOR

At our church, we focus intently on developing leaders, and lesson number one is that every prospective leader must honor senior leadership. You can't be a leader in our church if you fail to learn and apply this lesson. This isn't about a pastor's ego. Leaders must honor the pastor because their attitude is contagious. It permeates the entire congregation. It sets the tone for the whole church. Show me a church whose members disrespect the pastor, and I will be able to trace that disrespect to members of the leadership committee, board of elders, and other leaders.

It's important to note here that the disrespect might not be public, but it emerges in those little side conversations or around the dinner table at home. The private complaining bleeds into the fabric of a church and creates a tone and spirit of disrespect among the people.

The principle of honoring leadership applies to *anyone* who wants to be successful. You must honor the people in positions of authority in your life, on your job, in your business, and in any organizations you serve.

When I became the pastor at First Baptist, I researched some of the most successful churches in the country. I wanted to learn what made them succeed. I studied all kinds of churches. They had different worship styles, different policies, different organizational structures, and so on. But I found a common thread. Every thriving church deeply respected their pastor. They treated their pastor like God's mouthpiece into their lives—not as a celebrity or a rock star, but as a servant of God committed to integrity and strong character.

A church's leaders must have this mentality about their pastor. They shouldn't be critical and judgmental, always asking, "Why is he doing this and not *that*?" I should note that accountability and healthy, respectful feedback should be a hallmark of a pastor's relationship with the congregation. But constant gossiping, second-guessing, and criticizing is damaging and contagious, and church leaders should recognize this.

That's why elders, deacons, board members, and other leaders should demonstrate a healthy respect for the pastor. If you come to First Baptist Church of Glenarden and talk negatively about Pastor John K. Jenkins Sr., the mothers of the church will take you out back and beat you with their canes—in Jesus's name—because they have a healthy respect for their pastor. They will not tolerate anyone's disrespect.

People must learn to respect and honor the position of pastor, even if they do not like or agree with the person holding the position. And church leaders should reflect the pastor's spirit. What does it mean to have the pastor's spirit? It means the church leaders should do their jobs and respond to issues the way the pastor would, *not* according to their own preferences or viewpoints.

Leaders should always ask questions like these:

"How would the pastor want this task done?"
"What does the pastor say about this issue?"
"How can I model the pastor's spirit in this situation?"
"What has the pastor taught us, and how can we apply it to the problem at hand?"

Remember how Elisha asked for a double portion of Elijah's spirit? In 2 Kings 2:9 (NIV), Elisha said to Elijah, "Let me inherit a double portion of your spirit." That's what church leaders should want too—a double portion of their pastor's spirit.

Why is this so important? Because when people do what they *think* is best and disregard the spirit of their leadership, anarchy ensues. That's a problem. God calls us to emulate our pastors because that's a key element of being an effective leader and an effective church member. Of course, I say this with the expectation that we pastors lead in a way that *deserves* to be emulated, that we are diligent about earning and maintaining the respect of others.

I once asked the congregation to tell me what my spirit was. I was grateful that they listed all kinds of positive things. But then I turned that list into a challenge for them. "I expect you to have a double portion of my spirit," I said. "For instance, you have said that I am patient with people who are irrational or nasty. I expect you to be even *more* patient than I am."

DEVELOPING LEADERS

Character and leadership come naturally to some people, but others need help to develop in these areas. That's why we offer a variety of classes and other resources to help develop our leaders. For example, our leaders are required to participate in our Leadership Institute, which helps equip them to lead effectively. The Institute offers classes that teach people how to run meetings, how to deal with a person who is creating conflict, and how to move their ministry forward. We also teach our leaders how to motivate volunteers so our church has the participation and support we need.

We provide training in time management and financial management, both keys to making a leader effective. After all, if someone is going to be a leader responsible for managing budgets, they need to be able to manage their own money. We also teach strategies for growing a ministry. Every year we offer continuous training in all of the areas mentioned above.

And because our church continues to grow consistently, we repeat classes every few years so we are constantly training and equipping people to be leaders. I encourage you to do the same.

Chapter Fourteen

Resolve Conflict

When I became the pastor at First Baptist, I imme-diately encountered a challenge the church leaders needed me to address. This problem had affected the church for a long time, and as I began to peel back the layers, I discov-ered that the people at the heart of the matter were behaving in problematic ways. They were not administering a program correctly, and it was costing the church money.

My solution? End the program immediately. When I made that change, it sent some people into an uproar. The conflict that ensued was quite a sight to see. People were angry with me for the way I handled things, and they began talking about me among themselves. This bothered me because it felt like retaliation.

I realized, however, that I had a bigger platform than they did. I had the microphone. So, as people talked about me in meetings, I talked about them from the pulpit. I shouted things like, "You're going to hell!" In my anger, I thought that was the right way to fight back.

Then God took me to 2 Timothy, chapter 2, and started whipping my behind. Verse 24 says, "And the Lord's servant must not be quarrelsome but must be kind to everyone, able to teach, not resentful" (NIV).

This Scripture reminded me that I needed to be kind and gentle to everybody, not just the people who were kind to me and did what I wanted. Further, verse 25 of this passage in the NIV adds that opponents "must be gently instructed." (The New King James version says correction must be done "in humility.") This Scripture changed my life.

I realized I was not following God's will. I was not showing humility. I was not being patient. I was not correcting people the way God instructed. So, I repented before God, and I sat down with those opposing me and listened to them. I put myself in their shoes to see their perspective. And I saw that they were good people who meant no harm.

Their goals were noble, but their methods needed to change. As I listened, I understood their hearts better. This led me to reinstate the program, but with the changes needed to make it more effective and financially sound. That program has been going strong for thirty years now. What's more, some of my former adversaries are now among my greatest supporters in addition to holding key leadership roles in our church. It's amazing!

Every leader is going to face challenges and conflicts, and I pray that God will provide us the wisdom and courage to deal with them. God has an answer for all conflicts, but we must be willing to face them with honesty, humility, and fairness. Unfortunately, many people run from conflict because they lack the knowledge and experience to deal with it.

I recommend handling conflict according to Matthew 18:15–17, which instructs us to go directly to the offending person and point out his or her fault privately. This is what I teach at our church. And I provide guidelines for how to approach others in a conflict situation: what to say, how to listen, and how to bring resolution. Anyone can do this—there's no special anointing needed. All you need are a willing heart and a few key communication skills.

THE SBI METHOD

Let's dig deeper into the Matthew 18 passage. As noted above, the first step in conflict resolution is a direct and private conversation with the person who has sinned against you. The Bible is clear about avoiding discussions with others or holding a meeting to get outside feedback. Go to the person *alone* and try to resolve things.

Situation
Behavior
Impact

Most people avoid this commandment because they do not know what to say or they are uncomfortable with one-on-one confrontations. To help overcome these concerns, I teach the SBI model, which stands for situation, behavior, and impact.

Following this model, our first move is going to the person and identifying the *situation*. Specifically, what happened, or what keeps happening? Focus on the situation, not the person. Don't say things like . . .

"You never . . ."

"You always . . ."

"You shouldn't have . . ."

It's also important to consider the situation's *timing*, in every sense of that word. Choose the time for your conversation with wisdom and consideration. And point to a *specific time* when the problem occurred. You will enjoy much better results when you try to solve a problem, not attack or retaliate against a person, especially if that person feels ambushed or blindsided.

Next, you can move on to *behavior*. Tell the person what they have done and how it has created a problem. Focus on the behavior, something that can be observed. Don't make assumptions about someone's motives or the condition of his heart. That's a mistake. God knows everyone's hearts thoroughly, but He didn't give us that ability. When we judge someone's heart, we make an accusation that cannot be proven. We can't tell someone, "You don't love me" or "You want to hurt me." Such accusations are demonic, and we simply cannot treat others this way. Never assume someone's intentions. Address the actual behavior instead.

This brings us to the letter "I." Simply state how the

person's behavior *impacted* you. What were the results, and how did that make you feel?

Here's an example of how the SBI model works in real life: I might approach someone and say, "I saw you yesterday and said hello, but you didn't speak to me." In this one sentence, I have identified the situation and the behavior. Then I can move on to the impact. "Because you didn't acknowledge me, I am concerned you might be upset with me for some reason—or maybe I'm just not important to you." So, without making an accusation or attacking, I have opened up the possibility for a dialogue that can lead to resolving the matter.

Now, let's flip the script: What should we do when someone approaches *us* with their issue, their SBI?

THE LUVAA METHOD

The model I recommend is called LUVAA, which was developed by my spiritual son Pastor Keith Battle.

> **L**isten
> **U**nderstand
> **V**alidate
> **A**pologize
> **A**mend

The L stands for *listen*. That means I will focus on what the person is saying, not talk over him or her or start forming a rebuttal in my head. No. I'm going to listen to *everything* this person has to say.

The U stands for *understand*. When we strive to understand someone, we are saying, "I am going to put myself in your shoes and try to understand how you feel. I'm going to focus on you, not me. I'm will not talk over you or become defensive, because those things hinder understanding."

V is for *validate*. Validate the person and his or her feelings. This doesn't mean you must agree with how they feel, or that you need to like it. Just acknowledge that the feelings are real and they matter to the person in front of you.

The first A stands for *apologize*. And please don't say anything like "If I did anything to hurt you" or "If you were offended by what I said. . . ." Those are *not* apologies. That's not taking ownership of anything. Here is a real apology: "I was wrong, and I am sorry. Will you forgive me?" That question is key. It is vital to gain a sense of release from someone you have wronged.

I know that some of you might be thinking, *Do I really have to apologize if I have not done anything wrong?* To be a mature Christian, you must learn to accept the wrong, even though you might not *be wrong*. Why? Because sometimes this is what it takes to heal a relationship and move it forward. Sometimes we have to take the hit. After all, this is what Jesus did for us. He took the hit for us, even though he did nothing wrong.

The Scriptures teach us to agree with our adversaries *quickly*. Jesus modeled this for us. We should look to him and remember that relationships are valuable. It's worth taking the hit and apologizing to preserve something valuable, isn't it?

The final A stands for *amend*, in the sense of "put right."

Sometimes an apology isn't enough; sometimes we need to make amends to resolve a conflict or reconcile a wrongdoing. Think about your situation and what needs to be done to make things right. Identify the needed actions and follow through.

BUT WHAT ABOUT . . .

When I teach on this subject, it's common to hear "What about?" scenarios. For example, sometimes the person we have offended holds a perspective that is not based on facts. Does this mean we have to agree about something that simply isn't true?

No. In these cases, we might need to bring clarity to the situation—but only after we have devoted time and effort to listening and understanding. Then we can gently clarify any misunderstanding that might cloud the situation. This can be done without becoming defensive—or *offensive*.

Let's return to my earlier example, of someone walking right by me without acknowledging my greeting. When I describe my SBI, the person might inform me, "You know what? I'm sure I did fail to speak to you, and that wasn't my intention. I had just been notified about a personal emergency, and I was rushing to take care of it. I meant you no offense, and I'm sorry. Please forgive me."

This is a great example of someone respectfully clarifying the true nature of the situation, helping someone (me, in this case) better understand what was going on, and effectively resolving a conflict.

Conflict is uncomfortable to deal with, but it's important to deal with it quickly. Delaying things will make matters more uncomfortable, not less. Scripture is clear about this. Ephesians 4:26 warns us to avoid the sun going down on our wrath. Ignoring or "stuffing" anger only makes it grow. It spawns other problems like resentment, bitterness, and unforgiveness.

We focused on the importance of character in the previous chapter, but I want to note here that resolving conflict is a great way to build character.

Being a conflict resolver shows obedience to God, and it keeps issues from growing out of control. Conflict doesn't vanish on its own. It must be resolved.

Conflict is inevitable in a church or ministry. After all, God uses all kinds of people to get His work done, and that includes tough people, sensitive people, difficult people, strong-willed people, emotional people, and so on. We shouldn't regard such people as problems, but as those who can help build our character.

Ultimately, God is interested in us being more like Jesus, and Jesus dealt with all kinds of interpersonal conflicts. When you encounter a personal conflict, God wants you to learn something from it. So be a willing student and follow the biblical model for resolving each conflict.

Throughout this book, I have highlighted the importance of relationships. As I've said, relationships are the currency God uses to get his work done. If we claim to be Christians, we must handle life's conflicts and interpersonal challenges the way Christ instructs. I require all leaders in our church to be willing and able to communicate effectively with those who have conflicts. When someone approaches one of our leaders and says, "I need to talk to you," they need to sit down with that person (regardless of his or her position in the church) and talk things through. If someone is unwilling to do this, he or she cannot be a leader at First Baptist.

Handling conflict biblically is one of a Christian's hardest tasks. I know that it's difficult, and I don't know anyone who enjoys it. But if we will summon the courage to manage conflict God's way, we will see growth in our character, in our relationships, and in our ministries.

Part Four

Build a Connected Community

Chapter Fifteen

Provide Ministries for the Seasons of Life

I encourage every church to provide ministry to five key groups: children and youth, young adults, seniors, married and premarital couples, and singles.

Most pastors and ministry leaders understand the importance of serving young people. After all, they represent the church's next generation. If we fail to serve and nurture the next generation, our churches and other ministries won't grow.

It is rare but beautiful that our church has a children's pastor, a youth pastor, and a young adult pastor. Each of these life stages presents unique challenges and opportunities, and each has different ministry needs. But all of our youth know and understand our vision and mission (highlighted in Chapter 2). They know they are needed and valued, and this makes for a rewarding and amazing ministry experience. Our youth ministry prides itself in duplicating the vision and model of the adult church.

Our seniors are equally important. We need their knowledge and experience. The younger generations should learn all they can from the people who have gone before them. Leviticus 19:32 (NKJV) urges us to "rise before the gray headed and honor the presence of an old man. . . ." We honor our seniors when we make them a part of everything we do.

As for the married couples, they are the foundation of our families. We must offer married (and premarital) couples the resources and support they need to grow and thrive.

Now, let's look at each of these groups in more detail.

CHILDREN AND YOUTH

When I became pastor at First Baptist, my first hire was the youth pastor. This was a significant decision because at that time many African American churches didn't make hiring a full-time youth pastor a priority. Many hired a choir director or musical director or pianist/organist first. But what does that say about a church's priorities? I value music, of course, but serving our youth is *essential*.

Our church is living proof of this. The children who were ages five to ten years old when I became pastor are now in their thirties and forties. Many are still active in the church because we poured into them. We loved on them. We showed that we cared about them as people. We developed relationships with them. Because of our commitment to our youth—and the relationships we have built—we see many of them leave for college and then return to First Baptist and become active members after they graduate.

Researcher George Barna notes that a person who joins a church will stay connected if he or she develops *meaningful relationships* within the first six months.[9] I have seen this research proven time and time again at First Baptist. That's why we invest time in developing our young people and making meaningful connections with them. We've seen these connections endure—and even grow stronger—as younger generations grow into adulthood.

One way we cultivate our youth is by devoting the third Sunday of each month to them. Our children and teens take an active role in that worship service, and their parents (as well as other adults in their lives) show up in large numbers. In fact, Remix Sunday consistently draws the largest attendance, month after month. It's rewarding to see parents, grandparents, and neighbors supporting our youth who are part of the worship service. It underscores the fact that our youth know that they are valued, seen, and expected to lead. We prayerfully believe that youth who lead in church will become *adults* who stay in church—and lead in church.

Remix Sunday is a big evangelistic day for us, so I make sure the choir is ready. My sermon is evangelistic because when adults show up to support their children, that's a great time to welcome them to the kingdom. Additionally, we have learned that parents and other family members attend for reasons beyond supporting the youth. They are looking for answers. They want to know what the church can do for their families, so we place great emphasis on showing them how our church can meet their needs.

For example, today's youth are technology gurus. They are Instagram influencers, TikTokers, YouTubers, and digital-content creators. They make amazing videos that inform, entertain, and mobilize others all over the world. That's why our church has embraced digital discipleship. Because Generation Z (those between ten and twenty-five) grew up with technology, it was natural to empower them to lead from digital platforms. This became vital during the COVID-19 pandemic. Our youth ministry was able to continue weekly services, using slogans like "Shut In, But Not Shut Down," "Physical Distancing, Not Social Distancing," and "We May Be Insulated, But We Are Not Isolated."

Some of our virtual services were recorded; others went live on various platforms. Our youth created content for Motivational Monday, Testimony Tuesday, Workout Wednesday, Throwback Thursday, and so on. They led prayer calls and conducted virtual mental-health check-ins. They invited their unchurched friends to join them in small-group Zoom meetings and other pandemic-safe outreach events.

I should note that the pandemic forced us to face a question: What if we are preparing our youth for a church that no longer exists? That led to another, more important question: What if what we see as a problem for today's church is really God's *answer* for the church? Indeed, the pandemic helped our youth ministry realize the need to do real, relevant, and relational ministry on virtual platforms so we could serve youth who are not sharing our same physical space. During the pandemic, we saw an increase in attendance.

However, we also saw a decrease in the level of participation. Some of our youth (and also some adults) became spectators rather than active participants. This increased our efforts to empower our youth to not only serve one another but also to minister to our church at large. That's why our youth preside on Remix Sunday, as I noted earlier. They lead the praise and worship on the large platform. They answer the calls when someone is seeking salvation.

You might remember that I mentioned our altar-counselor certification process earlier in the book, and we have young people who are certified for this role. They receive the same training as the adults in our church. They wear badges that identify them, so a child or teen who comes forward can find a peer to help them. Our young people can also serve adults if needed.

What's more, a few of our teens have been trained to respond to anyone watching a service online who calls in asking for prayer or wanting to make a decision for Christ.

SENIORS

We've seen our ministry to seniors grow and develop over the years. First Baptist has always honored its seniors; however, there was a time when they were not deeply involved in the church's activities and ministries.

To address this deficit, I hired a full-time senior-care pastor, someone committed to serving seniors' needs and getting them actively involved in the church's life. We started by holding a weekly meeting for seniors. Today, our seniors are at the church every day for one reason or another. They volunteer for various tasks. They work in the nursery and participate in activities developed specifically for them. They take trips, play games, study the Bible, exercise, and connect with one another in the process.

For example, Seniors on the Go is designed for active adults fifty-five and up, whether they are retired, semi-retired, or still in the workforce full-time. They participate in fun outings like dinner shows, stage plays, and travel, and they also participate in community service and church outreach activities.

Senior Wednesday is a weekly fellowship event where members share their talents, wisdom, and experience with each other and with the community at large. Senior Wednesday also features speakers from the community who discuss relevant topics and share information and resources that will benefit our members in this age group. In this setting, our seniors have learned about housing options, wills and trusts, health and wellness, energy-efficiency programs, and food/nutrition assistance.

I encourage all churches to minister to seniors and focus on their needs. This is a great way to connect with them, disciple them, and give them opportunities to serve their church and community and to build relationships with other seniors.

YOUNG ADULTS

Our young adult ministry (which serves people eighteen to thirty-five) is another high priority for us for very good reasons. Young adults bring a valuable perspective to the church. Yes, their viewpoints might differ from those of the older generation, and this can make it hard for some churches to embrace them. But it's vital to listen to our young adults. They need a seat at the table, including church planning and strategy. Their voices need to be heard. Churches that fail to connect with their young adults put themselves at risk of a severe decline in the years to come.

Think about this in the business context: Companies that were successful fifty years ago have gone out of business because they failed to embrace new technology or new ideas. The church functions the same way. Our young adults are bringing new technology and new ideas to the table. Failing to listen to them and adopt some of their ideas will ultimately lead to a church's demise. Why? Because when young people realize they are not being respected or listened to, they leave. If this happens, who are we going to train to lead future generations? Without a base of young adults who are involved and invested in the church, what will the church's future look like?

This is why we have created an array of ministries and programs designed specifically for our young adults. We provide opportunities and outlets for them to express themselves and contribute to our church in meaningful and authentic ways. For example, our young adult ministry, ID, hosts an event called Checkpoint, a monthly Bible study designed for young adults. ID also provides a monthly event called The Gathering, a creative fellowship time that features roundtable discussions, prayer nights, poetry nights, and guest speakers who address relevant issues.

Through our College Connection program, our church's young adults transport local college students from their campuses to First Baptist every Sunday. After the service, the young adults host a fellowship time with the students. They enjoy a meal and engage in a thirty-minute discussion about the sermon or a college-relevant topic, such as financial aid.

We also provide an annual young adult conference, as well as Life Groups, where ten to twelve young adults spend time studying the Bible and discussing and experiencing life together.

Young adults enjoy community; they enjoy connecting with one another. That's why these groups are based on dialogue and sharing rather than preaching. In these group settings, participants can feel free to ask questions and express themselves honestly and openly.

Another way we engage our young adults is by allowing them to take the lead on our fifth Sunday service. This is an important cross-generational ministry opportunity for our church. Our young adults enjoy full control over that service, so they serve as presiders and lead the praise and worship. In fact, they coordinate *everything* for that service, and we allow them to be as creative as they like. This can mean dramatic lighting or nontraditional music. They might incorporate dance and drama into the service—anything to make it reflect their unique ideas and expressions of worship.

Another favorite cross-generational ministry is our Combined Choir, which combines the talents of all the FBC choirs, from the Sunbeam Choir (composed of kids five to eleven), the Chosen Generation Choir (for those ages twelve to seventeen), our Young Adult Choir, our Male Chorus, and everything in between. These choirs unite to sing a wide array of music—from traditional hymns to contemporary gospel—in a variety of settings.

MARRIED COUPLES AND PREMARITAL COUPLES

We also place great emphasis on serving our couples—those who are already married and those who are planning to marry. First Baptist has hired a couple who serve as full-time directors of our Couples Ministry, which reinforces the covenant of marriage. Married and engaged couples are ministered to through classes, counseling, workshops, panel discussions, social outings, and more. Everything we do is designed to build and maintain strong, healthy marriages.

MARRIED AND ENGAGED COUPLES

Here are a few key components of this ministry:

Our Couples Mentoring class consists of two twelve-week sessions that provide proven strategies, principles, and practices adopted from a conflict-resolution method called Round the Bases. One-on-one mentoring is also available.

Couples Focus studies last six to ten weeks and address the issues and concerns typically faced by today's married couples. These studies are available year-round, and they emphasize applying biblical principles to married life. Topics include remarriage, blended families, infidelity, and money management.

Couples 8@8 features small groups that provide accountability, spiritual growth, and relationship building. In this program's early days, four couples would convene one Saturday a month at eight o'clock in the evening. That's where the name came from. Today, each group decides when to meet. And some of the groups have more than eight people, as they have decided to add another couple or two to their numbers. The small-group setting allows couples to share and discuss God's Word and participate in activities in a more intimate, personal way than in large events. They also enjoy fun activities like bowling and dining out. Some couples have even vacationed together.

The goal is for each group to continue in perpetuity, so they can continue to build relationships and grow together spiritually. Currently, we have more than forty couple groups participating. A leader couple oversees the big picture, and each small group has an administrative leader who helps coordinate activities and communicates with the leader couple, the pastor, and other church leaders.

Like all of our ministries, our Couples Ministry strives to be relevant to the times. Our participation actually increased during the pandemic (to more than 5,000 couples) because we allowed people to participate via various online platforms and we focused on issues that were magnified during COVID-19 isolation, such as infidelity via the internet, online gambling, and pornography. And our classes are open to anyone.

Additionally, it is important to note that about 40 percent of our couples are "second timers," those in a second marriage due to death or divorce. And we recognize that some of today's marriages might be the first for one member of the couple and the third for the other. (It's worth mentioning that our second timers are our most active couples.)

I realize that the prospect of a devoted couples ministry can seem overwhelming to a small church. But consider what you do well and build on that—even if it's just one or two things. Don't be afraid to partner with other churches to provide more options if you see the need.

Remember that consistency is the key, not variety. It's the lack of *relationship* that draws people away from churches, not a lack of programs. Show today's couples you care and watch what happens.

A ministry for couples is vital for all churches, because if we can teach couples how to get along, we grow our churches by strengthening a key building block of a church (and a society): the family.

I frequently lead a series on marital relationships, and church attendance swells every time. Why? Because couples want and need to understand how to get along. Consider the divorce rate in your community, or the incidents of domestic abuse and unrest. It's clear that many couples don't know how to get along or communicate effectively. Simply put, they don't know how to be married.

That's one reason our Couples Ministry provides ongoing support for married duos, via mentor couples. These mentors are trained in biblical truths so they can help struggling couples or *any* couple wanting to strengthen their relationship.

> **It's the lack of *relationship* that draws people away from churches, not a lack of programs.**

Our mentors are not only well-trained, they also are seasoned couples who have been married for many years. They have survived the challenges that married couples face, so they are well-equipped to help others who face difficult times.

Beyond all of the above, we ensure that our couples spend time together *outside* of the church by organizing a variety of activities beyond our church campus. Our couples attend movies and plays, they go on cruises, go bowling, and enjoy a variety of other activities that allow them to connect with other couples, especially older, more seasoned couples.

Another highlight for this group is our annual retreat, usually held a few hours away from the church. This allows our couples to get away from the responsibilities of home and the job and truly relax and create memories together. We also host a popular Valentine's Day banquet. We combine this banquet with a "marriage tune-up" the day after, another part of our ongoing efforts to mentor couples and help them survive and thrive. Our couples enjoy these efforts so much that they invite other couples—their friends, family members, and coworkers—to participate. We have seen many couples join our church as a result.

It's hard to adequately describe how powerful this ministry has become. It's huge in our church, and we have seen so many couples grow spiritually and strengthen their family bonds. As a result, our church has grown stronger as well.

I hope you are inspired and energized by what you've read in this section. I encourage you to explore how you can serve the married couples in your church.

PREMARITAL COUPLES

As you might guess, we focus on ministering to our premarital couples, not just those who are already wed. We provide two premarital classes, and you can't get married in our church if you fail to complete both of them.

The first class is called "So You Think You Want to Get Married?" It lasts for ten weeks, which is longer than most premarital counseling programs. That's by design because this class helps people explore the Bible's values and instructions regarding marriage. It enables them to validate their call to marriage and discern whether they should marry the person they are dating.

This class emphasizes hearing God's voice and receiving clear instruction on the life-altering decision to marry. Participants also learn about realistic expectations for marriage, receiving a parental blessing, and finances for couples. For example, we encourage premarital couples to share credit scores with one another and be completely honest about their respective financial situations.

By the end of the class, participants should be able to answer this question: "Is this my season for marriage?" Every year, several hundred people take this class. We draw lots of people from other churches in our community because those churches don't offer anything like it.

Clearly, more churches need to support their premarital couples and invest resources into serving them. I encourage you to explore how your church can meet the need for premarital classes and counseling.

Our other premarital class, "Becoming One," also runs for ten weeks. Couples can take this class only after completing "So You Think You Want to Get Married?"

Our goal for this follow-up class is to give engaged couples (or any couple who feels confident that God is leading them toward marriage) a blueprint for developing a Christ-centered marriage. We cover topics like marital myths, the meaning of marriage vows, effective communication, resolving conflict, and sex. We believe that too many couples get married without adequate preparation and communication. That's why this class and its predecessor are requirements for any couple wanting to get married in our church.

SINGLES

The landscape of our country has changed tremendously over the years, and this has impacted the church in many ways. Our church, like many others, now serves a growing number of single men and women.

In the early 1960s, the average age for marriage in the United States was 20.3 for women and 22.8 for men. Today, according to Statista, people are waiting longer to get married. The average age is now 30 for men and almost 28 for women.[10]

Men and women are delaying marriage for several reasons. Some want to finish their education, join the military, or focus on their careers. In other cases, men and women find themselves single after divorce or the death of a spouse. Whatever the situation, modern singles want to feel included and accepted by their church family. This is especially true for those who struggle with their sense of self-worth as a result of being single.

And it's important for the church to foster and develop well-rounded singles who desire to serve the Lord wholeheartedly, without distraction, while pursuing their God-given purpose in life. Far too often, singles are reluctant to pursue their dreams because of societal pressures to make marriage their priority. In other cases, a single man or woman might think their goals will be more achievable with a supportive spouse by their side.

Our church's singles ministry seeks to help members to

grow spiritually, connect socially, and serve passionately—in the church as well as the community. Our ministry hosts monthly gatherings that cover a variety of topics, ranging from finances, health and wellness, dating, starting a business, and much more. Each topic is explained and discussed from a biblical perspective. We also offer a nightly prayer call and a variety of monthly outreach activities and outings. Our singles go bowling, attend professional sports events, enjoy an outdoor movie night, and so on.

The ultimate goal of this ministry is to teach singles to lead godly lives and find contentment in being single, whether their ultimate goal is to find a spouse soon, at some point in the distant future, or, perhaps, remain single until God shows them otherwise.

One final note about our singles ministry. We embrace both dating and courtship. We know that most people begin romantic relationships through dating. However, once a worthy candidate for a deeper relationship emerges, we encourage a transition to courting over dating. Courting couples focus on helping one another discern God's will for their lives. In courtship, a couple strives to determine if their respective skills, temperaments, and character are compatible in helping them achieve God's purpose for their life, both as individuals and as a duo.

CULTIVATING RELATIONSHIPS

Back in Chapter 9 (which focused on evangelism), I shared the story of my youngest daughter, who played sports not because she enjoyed them, but because she enjoyed the relationships with her friends who played sports. I return to that lesson now, because relationships are a focal point of all of our ministries.

In each of the ministries I have described in this chapter, relationship building is critical in keeping people connected with our church. Like it or not, people shop for churches like they shop for cars. They want something that appeals to their lifestyle and meets their needs. They want to feel cared about as individuals, not just as part of one more statistic in a church.

People's lifestyles and needs can shift as they go through the stages of life, and that's why it's vital for churches to offer something for everyone at every life stage. Appeal to the specific needs of various groups and watch your church grow.

I have highlighted five key ministries in this chapter, but there are many other opportunities to meet people where they are in their seasons of life and to help them grow spiritually and cultivate relationships. (For example, is there a military base in your community? Is there a large population representing a specific ethnic group?)

> It's vital for churches to offer something for everyone at every life stage.

Some of First Baptist's other ministries serve people with special needs, caregivers, widows, and the hearing impaired. We also have a Spanish-speaking ministry. The key is to make your ministries relatable so people can identify with them, get involved, and start building relationships.

Relationships are important and powerful, but they don't happen automatically. They must be built and maintained. That's why we must focus on teaching people how to get along with one another. Let's teach them how to resolve their conflicts.

Throughout our church, we teach how to develop relationships. That is why we have a full-time children's pastor, a full-time youth pastor, a full-time seniors pastor, a full-time young adult director, and full-time couples directors. Their job is to cultivate relationships with those they serve and provide godly direction.

Church is all about relationships over programs. Yes, we can and should offer programs, but if those programs don't create and build *relationships*, people won't stay in our churches.

Chapter Sixteen

Empower Your Ministries to Serve the Community

As I mentioned back in Chapter 7, when I became First Baptist's pastor in 1989, we had thirty-two auxiliaries (called clubs) that held thirty-two anniversary celebrations each year. I realized we needed to try something new. I invited Dr. Harold Trammell, who was pastor at nearby Mount Jezreel Baptist Church, to help our church better understand the work of ministries.

We were doing "church work," but not the actual work of the church. Our clubs weren't striving to impact people's lives. Instead, they were focused on their respective anniversaries. They spent time planning for their celebrations, they celebrated, and then waited for the day when they could celebrate again.

Things changed with Dr. Trammell's training. During the week-long conference he led for us, he drew a large pie chart. He asked us for the names of our clubs and made each one of them a slice of the pie. Next, he drew a similar chart and asked us to list the problems our community was facing. Those problems became the slices on the second chart. Finally, he asked us, "What are your clubs doing to address these problems in your community?"

Silence fell over the room. No one could offer an example. The sanctuary was carpeted, but you still could hear a pin drop.

The results of Dr. Trammell's efforts were life changing. After the seminar, the first thing we did was drop the term "club" and adopt the term "ministry." Next, each ministry was assigned to find a need in the community and determine how to meet it. Over the course of a year, each ministry found its need, its niche, and started serving. It was amazing!

We were doing "church work," but not the actual work of the church.

Dr. Trammell returned one year later, and he re-created his two pie charts. He asked the same question he had posed before. But this time, people stood up and offered reports such as, "Our ministry started serving in a nursing home," or, "We are currently ministering in area prisons." Another person offered, "Our ministry discovered a family that was struggling, so we prepared dinner for them every day for a month." People started jumping up like popcorn. When it was all over, there wasn't a dry eye in the house.

And that wasn't the end of the story. "I am in this church

today," someone volunteered, "because one of your ministries came to me and served my family." Others in the room shared similar stories of how one of our ministries had made a difference in their lives and the lives of people they cared about. This experience marked a shift from tradition-bound customs to applying new principles based on biblical doctrine.

We had readjusted our focus from inward to outward, and it changed the course of our church forever. Most important, we focused on incorporating outreach into every ministry. Each ministry, new or old, was responsible for finding needs in the community and serving those needs.

Today we have 120 ministries, and each one serves a specific community need. Mention a need, and it's highly likely that we have a ministry for it—from surviving sexual abuse to dealing with cancer. Because our ministries meet so many needs, I know that if our church ever ceased to exist, our community would profoundly miss our presence. (This is a great litmus test for any church, by the way.)

> **If our church ever ceased to exist, our community would profoundly miss our presence.**

I won't list all 120 ministries, but here are a few examples:

We have a ministry that supports families experiencing infertility or who need support in the adoption process. For example, we have partnered with other organizations and ministries to provide seminars about adoption, as well as foster care and infertility.

We have a ministry that supports women dealing with the devastating challenges they face in the wake of an abortion decision. "Beauty for Ashes," which began as an eight-week Bible study in 2007, is now a nine-month program. In it, women learn to embrace how God feels about life in general and the tragic sin of abortion in particular. We focus on a foundational relationship with Jesus, as the key to finding healing, forgiveness, and empowerment.

Our Turning Point ministry offers a safe and healthy environment to help people facing life-controlling issues such as substance abuse, addiction, anger management, and pornography. This ministry offers help in small-group settings, and there are separate classes and programs for adults and youth ages thirteen to seventeen. A related ministry (a small-group study titled Samson's Dilemma) helps men free themselves from sexual temptation and build godly boundaries in their lives.

We go to prisons and minister to those who are incarcerated, and we support their families as they deal with their own unique challenges. We take seriously Jesus's command to visit those in prison (Matt. 25:36). That's why our Prison Ministry goes behind bars to minister to men, women, and youth, sharing God's Word through preaching, witnessing, and written correspondence.

We have local and national missions that share love, hope, and resources with people in need. For example, our Feed the Hungry ministry provides nutritious meals and prayer to our local homeless population and to anyone without access to the nutrition they need.

We minister to the deaf community by providing interpreters who can help bring them the Word of God. Our Deaf Ministry provides interpreters for all worship services and special events using American Sign Language (ASL).

Our Spanish ministry translates our services and classes so we can connect with, serve, and disciple our Spanish-speaking community. We want every church member and visitor to be able to understand and apply God's Word. Spanish translation is available for our Sunday noon worship services, Communion services, Tuesday-night Bible studies, and a variety of our special events.

We have a ministry that helps families with special needs. We provide multisensory classrooms and inclusive buddies for our Sunday school classes and other educational settings because we want to ensure everyone can learn about God's love. This includes providing support groups for parents and other caregivers as well as childcare for special-needs children so the adults in their lives can have some time to rest and recharge.

I urge you to find ways your church can reach out to your community. We allocate some of our budget to support all of our ministries. You can do the same, even if your church is small. You don't need a huge budget to do outreach. If your budget lacks the funds, appeal to your congregation and to your community at large. You will be amazed by how many people will give of their resources, time, and talents to reach out and meet needs.

I want to close this chapter with a key truth: Sometimes you don't need money in the budget; you just need some people who are willing to serve in any way they can. That's how we got started. Several people donated money or goods to the church. Others simply showed up and said, "How can I serve?"

For example, our church learned about the plight of some homeless people who were living on the streets. We found apartments for them and raised enough money to pay rent for a year. We furnished the apartments with donations. We clothed the people with donations. And people donated groceries every month.

In addition to asking for help from your church and community, look for ways your church's various ministries can collaborate and do outreach together. We have found this pooling of resources, time, and people power to be very effective. I believe this synergy can work for you too as you seek to make an impact on your community and beyond.

Chapter Seventeen

Establish a Separate Nonprofit Entity

Some pastors and ministry leaders don't realize that many businesses and government agencies want to help them, but there are barriers and conditions related to this assistance. For example, certain organizations are wary of donating money directly to a church because they want to avoid controversy or appearing to favor one church or denomination over others. In other cases, companies or agencies are bound by restrictions that don't allow them to donate to a church.

Fortunately, we can provide a path for organizations who want to support our work by creating a separate nonprofit entity. This way, businesses can contribute to your nonprofit without giving directly to your church, and government agencies can form partnerships with your nonprofit—partnerships they couldn't establish with a church or ministry.

This arrangement also satisfies the reporting requirements some organizations follow because nonprofits are fully
transparent, meaning their financials are published. A nonprofit must publish financial and tax information that any
business or government agency can review to assess the nonprofit's financial stability, as well as its ability to use funds and
other resources effectively.

Before we proceed, I must note that chasing grants or
donations is *not* the right reason to form a nonprofit. Our
motives should be higher than that. Besides, it's getting
harder and harder to find a partner who will simply write
you a check. That's why I encourage *partnerships*, which you
can build through relationships. A partnership can be just as
beneficial as a donation (if not more so).

Our church established a nonprofit 501(c)3 corporation
called SHABACH! Ministries, Inc., which comprises three
divisions: Education, Community Services, and Administrative
(the operational division that oversees the other two).

The Education division includes our school, SHABACH!
Christian Academy, which is shaping young lives for the
Kingdom of God. This academy serves students from kinder-
garten through eighth grade. We also provide a preschool, a
K–12 homeschool option, and a program that provides before-
and after-school care and activities.

SHABACH is a private school, but our before/after services are open to public school students. Most private schools
serve only their own students, but we want to open our doors
to the whole community. We want to provide services so many
kids and their parents truly need.

Our Community Services division provides important

resources to needy people throughout our area. We provide food, clothing, employment assistance, and more. One of this division's major outreaches is our SHABACH! Emergency Resource Center, which operates from our church's Empowerment Center. From this building, we serve almost 100,000 people every year. These people are referred to us by agencies like the Department of Social Services, the Veterans Administration, and the Department of Aging.

Additionally, we partner with agencies like the Department of Agriculture to offer groceries to needy families. In most cases, these families can receive nonperishable food items from us without providing detailed personal information. When there are government shutdowns or furloughs, we provide the affected families with groceries. The testimonies we receive from those we serve are incredible. They say things like, "Your organization was the first one to treat us with dignity and respect."

I'll never forget our efforts to serve a police officer who was on disability. When her disability income expired, she came to us for food. Eventually, she got back on her feet, and today she is one of our volunteers!

Another outreach within Community Services is our Career Services Department, which provides employment-readiness programs that help people build skills like resume writing. We also help people master the job application and job interview processes. It would be difficult to tally all of the testimonies we have received about how these services have helped people find employment.

To help us offer the best possible service, we have established relationships with several employers with hard-to-fill positions.

These jobs require people of high character, so we offer special-ized courses in character development.

Once a year, we hold a career fair, featuring employers from the public and private sectors. We provide rooms for job interviews, and many attendees get hired on the spot. We also offer a youth summer employment program. Our church and our nonprofit combine forces to employ area youth for six weeks each summer.

WINNING PARTNERSHIPS AND AFFILIATIONS

We also partner with organizations to offer certifications in CPR and Mental Health First Aid. The mental health training has become very important, as mental-health needs in our com-munity continue to escalate. People who receive this certification are prepared to help someone suffering a mental health crisis, working with them and keeping them calm and safe until profes-sional assistance arrives. People who have completed this course have been able to make an immediate impact in our community.

As I write this chapter, we are creating a health center to provide education and health screenings and evaluations—specifically designed for the economically challenged.

To provide even more local support, we created a Commu-nity Services Coordinator position, and that person visits the apartment complexes in neighborhoods around the church, looking for needs to be met. Our coordinator quickly became the face of the church and a go-to person for the residents in the complexes. She created a resource guide, which gives people vital information on whom to contact for a variety of services and assistance. We have also donated supplies to children at the local community center, and we continually look for opportunities to share health and hope with our neighbors.

In short, our nonprofit divisions are providing significant help to people who need it.

I urge you to consider how you can expand your church's reach and form impactful partnerships through a nonprofit entity. Of course, churches establishing nonprofits should consider each partnership *carefully*. As I noted earlier, a partnering company or government agency may have certain requirements or restrictions you must follow. Take the time to fully vet the organization. Be aware of all the pros and cons before you form a partnership.

Additionally, be careful when setting up your nonprofit's structure and finances. A church and its nonprofit are *separate* entities, so seek the advice of a professional to ensure you are properly handling the nonprofit's governance and finances and complying with all rules and regulations.

I realize that the idea of creating a nonprofit can seem daunting, especially for smaller churches. We experienced concerns when we started our nonprofit in 1996. But I encourage you to remember the words of Zechariah 4:10 (NCV): "The people should not think that small beginnings are unimportant." The Living Bible paraphrase puts it this way: "Do not despise this small beginning, for the eyes of the Lord rejoice to see the work begin."

Scripture encourages us to be willing to start small. That's what we did. In our early days, we relied primarily on volunteers to get the work done. And we weren't embarrassed to reach out to larger churches for help. I urge you to follow this example.

Another challenge for a smaller church (or *any* church) considering a nonprofit is where to begin. To help you answer this question, I want to remind you of my advice from Chapter 2 about developing a vision and mission statement. I noted that your personal and organizational vision and mission should spring from a sense of passion, a sense of purpose and burden.

This holds true for your nonprofit as well. If you were to ask me, "Where should we start with our nonprofit?" I would answer, "What is your church passionate about?" The answer to that question might be your best litmus test.

This brings us to another key element of starting a nonprofit. Yours should have its own distinctive vision and mission statement. These statements should complement those of your church, but they should be specific to the separate entity. For example, SHABACH's vision statement is "To develop dynamic communities for generations to come, by meeting the need, giving hope and teaching to soar."

And here is the mission statement: "To empower families, individuals, youth, and children through stellar education and loving engagement, which cultivates exemplary character, a lifelong love of learning, and creates a healthier community today and tomorrow."

For more information on our nonprofit, please visit our website: smionline.org. I know you will find further details and inspiration there—including ideas on how to create your nonprofit's website.

Epilogue

As we near the end of this book, I hope you have come to appreciate two things:

1. Growing an effective ministry is deeply rewarding.
2. Growing an effective ministry can be very difficult.

As we've seen, those of us who lead churches face a variety of issues, challenges, and personality clashes along the way. I wish I could tell you that these obstacles can be avoided, but that doesn't reflect reality. That's why I've shared so many of my own challenges and how I dealt with them. Sometimes we can't avoid a problem; we have to address it. And I truly believe you will be better equipped to face whatever comes your way—and achieve positive outcomes—if you apply the principles in this book.

However, as you apply this book to your ministry and life, please remember the importance of accountability and personal support. As I have noted more than once in these pages, every pastor needs a pastor. Our effectiveness as leaders is limited if we pour ourselves into the lives of others but have no one to nourish and counsel us. We are human beings, after all, not bottomless wells.

We face challenges in our spiritual development and in our personal lives—including our relationships with spouses, children, and other family members. We need someone to talk to about these challenges.

Facing issues and problems is a routine part of leading a ministry, so we need regular counsel and accountability to keep our minds and spirits healthy and strong.

I am a pastor who has a pastor: Bishop T. D. Jakes. I also have friends and professional peers who hold me accountable and help me walk in the grace God has given me for my assignment. That accountability and support have made all the difference for me. I wish the same for you.

Every pastor needs a pastor.

I wrote this book to share our story at First Baptist Church of Glenarden—the ups and the downs—and to educate and encourage other pastors and ministry leaders. I hope and pray that something I have shared has connected with you and inspired you.

I pray all of our churches can be healthier and more effective. I believe we can make a difference if pastors and laypeople work as a team, doing ministry together. Let's learn to cooperate and avoid fighting among ourselves, within our churches, or *between* our churches. I don't want First Baptist to compete with other churches in our community, and I hope you feel the same way about your church or ministry.

If we commit ourselves to building effective ministries, God can and will give us grace to grow. He will empower each of our churches to serve the needs of our communities, all for his glory.

Afterword

There were giants on the earth in those days. . . .
Those were the mighty men who were of old, men of renown.
—Genesis 6:4

We praise God for the ancestors upon whose shoulders we stand. They were truly giants on the earth, mighty individuals of old, and persons of renown. Because they were, we are. But due to the passage of time, the fabrications and long view of history, and the inability to have face-to-face contact, physical communication, or an up-close view of heroes and heroines of the distant past, we sometimes bestow upon them a legendary status that makes their deeds and accomplishments seem impossible to duplicate or surpass.

However, what the creative genius and omnipotent power of our triune God has done before, God can do again. Genesis, the first book of the Bible, states, "In the beginning God created the heavens and the earth. The earth was without form, and void; and darkness was on the face of the deep. And the Spirit of God was hovering over the face of the waters" (Gen. 1:1–2).

In Revelation, the last book of the Bible, the visionary John writes, "Now I saw a new heaven and a new earth, for the first heaven and the first earth had passed away. Also there was no more sea" (Rev. 21:1).

What Almighty God does with the heavens and the earth, he also does with human life and human greatness. Giants and mighty persons of renown were God's gifts in the past. Their bright lights provided us a foundation upon which we build. Today, God also provides mighty persons. Their examples inspire and instruct us. They serve as role models and mentors for future generations. John Jenkins is the living embodiment of the truth that giants and persons of renown still breathe, talk, walk, teach, preach, and serve among us.

We are blessed and privileged with opportunities to personally know, laugh with, talk to, and observe firsthand the giants who move among us, spreading courage and character, holiness and humility, integrity and inspiration, knowledge and kindness, love and life, salvation and a smile, truth and tenderness, vision and virtue. John Jenkins, the author of this book, is such a giant among us.

Meeting and getting to know Pastor John Jenkins, observing him as a husband and feeling his pride and joy when he speaks about his children, witnessing the dynamism and power of his ministry, and being inspired and enlightened by his humble demeanor and unfeigned faith have been some of the greatest blessings and opportunities of my life. I thank God for the privilege of knowing Pastor Jenkins and the sainted queen of ebon hue who is his life companion and wife, Lady Trina Jenkins.

Those of us who admire and follow his ministry have

often scratched our heads and asked, "How does he do it?" How does one return as pastor to the medium-sized traditional church of one's youth and transform it into one of the largest, fastest-growing, best-respected, and most financially solvent megachurches in the nation? With John Jenkins, we know how some things have happened in his life and ministry: They are the result of his unwavering commitment to what truly matters. With John Jenkins, integrity matters! Faithfulness to one's vows matters! An uncompromising commitment to the Word of God matters! The needs of people and the plight of the community matter! The kingdom of God matters!

To John Jenkins, a personal, saved relationship with the Lord Jesus Christ matters! Being filled with the Holy Spirit matters! Biblical stewardship and sound financial management matter! Manifesting the fruit of the Spirit matters! Being a true pastor—a true shepherd over the flock of Christ and committed to its care—matters! John Jenkins is not a pastor merely by title; he is a pastor indeed.

While many of us who know him understand the personal qualities and characteristics that undergird his stellar leadership, we lack knowledge of the inner workings of his ministry's administration. This book opens the curtain and allows us to see his administrative practices and how he applies the principles that guide him in building and managing a vibrant and ever-expanding institution: the church, the body of Christ.

Thank you, Pastor John Jenkins, for being generous with your gifts and knowledge. Thank you for sharing with us how you do what you do. Thank you for helping so many of us understand how to use biblical principles to build, manage, maintain, and expand God's kingdom, as well as institutional infrastructures.

When one thinks about Pastor John Jenkins and the mighty ministry that the grace and power of God have empowered him to build in Jesus's name, these words of our Lord become especially real to us: "The kingdom of heaven is like a mustard seed, which a man took and sowed in his field, which indeed is the least of all the seeds; but when it is grown it is greater than the herbs and becomes a tree, so that the birds of the air come and nest in its branches" (Matt. 13:31–32).

Thank you, Pastor John Jenkins, for your mustard-seed, tree-growing, and forest-producing ministry. Most of all, thank you for being a giant and mighty person of renown in our times, who daily lays out a righteous foundation for generations to come. Peace!

REV. DR. WILLIAM D. WATLEY
Senior Pastor, Saint Philip African Methodist
Episcopal Church, Atlanta, GA

Acknowledgments

I extend my gratitude to the leaders and members of First Baptist Church of Glenarden, who have followed my leadership and helped build a powerful ministry that has impacted a community in a significant way.

I am also grateful to those who have served as mentors and teachers in my life. To Bishop T. D. Jakes, thank you for your spiritual covering and the many hours of coaching and mentoring that you have provided to me over the years. You have blessed me and those I serve beyond description!

I thank the late Dr. Harold Trammell for teaching me and our ministry how to impact a community.

I thank those who contributed to bringing this book to fruition. Thank you, Bishop Timothy J. Clarke, for entrusting me to share these truths with those you serve and for providing me with the recording that helped me create this book.

Dr. William Watley, thank you for believing I could make a difference in the lives of other pastors and leaders. Thank you for relentlessly pressing me to put these teachings into book form!

ACKNOWLEDGMENTS

To Dr. Jasmin Sculark, thank you for contributing your time and ideas to this project.

To Jennifer Westbrook (jenwestwriting.com) and Tressa Smallwood of Life Changing Books, thank you for your editing and your assistance in getting this book published.

To Georgina Agyekum Manzano, thank you for your support, and for the connections that have helped me publish this book.

Thanks to Todd Hafer and Tom Dean for their significant contributions to making this book a reality. Without your support, advise, and work, this book could not have been published!

I wish to thank my six children, Sarah, Joshua, Ana, Jimmy, Natalie, and Johnny, for sharing their father with the church and the world as I learned and practiced leading a growing church.

And last, but certainly not least, I thank my incredible wife, Trina Jenkins, for her faithful love, encouragement, and support.

Sample Code
of Conduct

First Baptist Church of Glenarden (FBCG) believes it is important that it be clear with its staff about its expectation that they uphold the highest standards of Biblical conduct, personally and professionally.

FBCG is a Christian organization, committed to the advancement of Christian principles, and establishes a Code of Conduct reflective of its belief.

I agree that, as part of the qualifications for this position, I am a "born-again" Christian who knows the Lord Jesus Christ as Savior (John 3:3, 1 Peter 1:23). I accept without verbal or mental reservations First Baptist Church of Glenarden's Code of Conduct, and am committed to upholding it.

I agree to manifest by daily example the highest Christian virtue serving as a Christian role model (1 Timothy 4:12) both in and out of my employment with the First Baptist Church of Glenarden to all persons I come into contact with (Luke 6:40), and fellow employees. I agree to be a role model in judgment, dignity, respect, and Christian living. I acknowledge that this includes, but is not limited to, the refraining from such activities as the use of alcoholic beverages, tobacco, illicit drugs, and the use of vulgar and profane language (Col. 3:17; Titus 2:7–8; 1 Thess. 2:10; 1 Thess. 5:18, 22–23; and James 3:17–18).

FBCG believes that God's design for the gift of sexuality is that it is to be exercised and enjoyed only within the covenant relationship of marriage between one man and one woman. We believe that it is God's intention that those who enter marriage shall seek, in mutual; love and respect. To live as one man and one woman, in Christian fidelity as long as both shall live.

FBCG believes that God has specifically and expressly condemned sexual intercourse outside of the marriage covenant. This prohibition applies to married persons committing adultery, to sexual relationships between unmarried men and women, and because God intends that the sexual relationship to be between male and female, to homosexual practice. We believe that it is God's expectation that the unmarried shall live pure and celibate lives refraining from sexual intimacy.

I agree to accept First Baptist Church of Glenarden's interpretation of Biblical standards for my sexual behavior. That any sexual misconduct—including, but not limited to—premarital, extramarital, or homosexual activity; sexual harassment; use or viewing of pornographic material or websites; and sexual abuse of children is forbidden and violates the employment requirement of being a Christian role model. I agree that such behaviors are grounds for immediate dismissal from my position.

I also agree that the unique roles of the male and female are clearly defined in Scripture, and that Romans 1:24–32 condemns the homosexual lifestyle (Rom. 12:1–2; 1 Cor. 6:9–20; Eph. 4:1–11, 5:3–5; 1 Thess. 4:3–8; 1 Tim. 4:12; 2 Tim. 2:19–22; 1 Peter 1: 15–16; 2:15–17; 1 John 3:1–3).

Although employment with the First Baptist Church of Glenarden is based on mutual consent and both the employee and the First Baptist Church of Glenarden have the right to terminate employment at will, with or without cause or advance notice. We have the right to decide on the appropriate action. We may consider: 1) the seriousness of your conduct, 2) your employment record, 3) your ability to correct the conduct, 4) actions we have taken for similar conduct by others, and 5) how your action affects the ministry and other circumstances. The First Baptist Church of Glenarden reserves the right to terminate any employee for reasons not stated in this handbook or for no reason at all.

IMMEDIATE REMOVAL OR ACTION

An employee may be discharged immediately for violating Church policies. Examples of reasons considered justification for immediate action include, but are not limited to:

1. Revealing confidential information concerning the Church members, employees, or guests.

2. Stealing Church property, co-workers property, or any other person's property.

3. Refusing or deliberately failing to carry out a reasonable instruction of your supervisor.

4. Intentional falsification of an employment application, timesheet, expense claim, or other Church documents.

5. Using Church equipment, personnel, or facilities to falsify documents or information.

6. Failure to get along with co-workers to the point that morale and productivity suffer.

7. Failure to follow the work rules.

8. Violation or disregard of an established security policy or practice of the ministry's security guidelines.

9. Professional or personal misconduct detrimental to the rights or safety of co-workers or members.

10. Failure to report for work without calling or without an excused absence.

11. Behavior indicating abuse of alcohol or controlled substances, either illegal or prescribed.

12. Personal conduct of a verbally or physically abusive nature.

13. Expiration/revocation or inability to demonstrate required licensure/registration/certification.

14. Indictment or conviction of a felony.

15. Excessive tardiness or unauthorized absences.

16. Arguing and/or fighting with co-workers, members, or guests.

17. Using or possessing alcohol or illegal drugs at work.

18. Using abusive language at work.

19. Coming to work under the influence of alcohol or illegal drugs.

20. Failing to carry out reasonable job assignments.

21. Violating Church rules and/or Biblical Principles adopted by the Church.

22. Unlawful discrimination or harassment.

23. Possessing any unlawful weapon on the work sites. An unlawful weapon includes gun, knife or any device prohibited by the ministry to be brought on the premises.

24. Using Church property or equipment for the employee's personal use without the prior consent of the Church.

25. Sexual misconduct in violation of Biblical principles described in the Handbook, this Code, or those that are in violation of federal, state, and local law.

It should be stressed that the above items are examples of serious misconduct, and the list is not intended to be all inclusive. In these cases the First Baptist Church of Glenarden's Church Administrator must be contacted before any action is taken.

I agree to attempt to resolve differences with others (fellow-workers, administration) by following the Biblical pattern of Matthew 18:15–17. Should the employee have unresolved issues with the employer after utilizing the Matthew 18 principle, I and the employer agree to be bound by the First Baptist Church of Glenarden Dispute Resolution Agreement in an attempt to resolve issues and bring reconciliation.

Persons hired with the First Baptist Church of Glenarden must acknowledge their agreement with this statement and commitment to abide by it.

I affirm that I have read and will abide by the Code of Conduct Statement.

Notes

1. Megan Brenan, "Nurses Retain Top Ethics Rating in U.S., but Below 2020 High," Gallup.com, January 10, 2023, https://news.gallup.com/poll/467804/nurses -retain-top-ethics-rating-below-2020-high.aspx. Members of the clergy were first measured by Gallup in 1977 and were frequently among the most-respected professions until 2002. The clergy's high / very high ethics ratings fell to 50 percent in 2009 and have been declining since 2012. The most recent rating of 34 percent is the lowest ever recorded.

2. Aaron Earls, "5 Current Church Attendance Trends You Need to Know," Lifeway.com, February 2, 2022, https:// research.lifeway.com/2022/02/02/5-current-church -attendance-trends-you-need-to-know/. See also Aaron Earls, "Most Teenagers Drop Out of Church When They Become Young Adults," Lifeway.com, January 15, 2019, https://research.lifeway.com/2019/01/15/most -teenagers-drop-out-of-church-as-young-adults/.

3. Pew Research Center, "Mobile Fact Sheet: Internet/

Broadband, Social Media," PewResearch.org, April 7, 2021, https://www.pewresearch.org/internet/fact-sheet/mobile/.

4. L. Ceci, "How Much Time on Average You Do You Spend on Your Phone on a Daily Basis?" Statista.com, June 14, 2022, https://www.statista.com/statistics/1224510/time-spent-per-day-on-smartphone-us/.

5. Emily A. Vogels, Risa Gelles-Watnick, and Navid Massarat, "Teens, Social Media and Technology 2022," PewResearch.org, August 10,2022, https://www.pewresearch.org/internet/2022/08/10/teens-social-media-and-technology-2022/. See also Brooke Auxier and Monica Anderson, "Social Media Use in 2021," PewResearch.org, April 7, 2021, https://www.pewresearch.org/internet/2021/04/07/social-media-use-in-2021/.

6. Erin Duffin, "How Often Do You Attend Church or Synagogue—at Least Once a Week, Almost Every Week, about Once a Month, Seldom, or Never?" Statista.com, September 30, 2022. See also Barna Group, "State of the Church 2020," Barna.com, March 4, 2020, barna.com/stateofthechurch.

7. Jeffrey M. Jones, "U.S. Church Membership Falls Below Majority for First Time," Gallup.com, March 29, 2021, https://news.gallup.com/poll/341963/church-membership-falls-below-majority-first-time.aspx.

8. John Maxwell, "Character: Who We Are on the Inside," blog post, JohnMaxwell.com, April 23, 2013, https://www.johnmaxwell.com/blog/character-who-we-are-on-the-inside/.

9. Barna Group, "5 Reasons Millennials Stay Connected to Church," Barna.com, September 17, 2013, https://www.barna.com/research/5-reasons-millennials-stay-connected-to-church/.

10. Erin Duffin, "Estimated Median Age of Americans at Their First Wedding in the United States from 1998 to 2021, by Sex," Statista.com, October 12, 2022, https://www.statista.com/statistics/371933/median-age-of-us-americans-at-their-first-wedding. See also Paul Hemez, "Distributions of Age at First Marriage, 1960–2018," National Center for Family & Marriage Research, Bowling Green, OH, April 6, 2021 (updated), Family Profile no. 9, 2020, https://doi.org/10.25035/ncfmr/fp-20-09.